Brain Dancing

and the Solutions Approach to Capacity Enhancement

Patrick T. Magee

Published by Magee Research
Bellevue, Washington USA

Editor: Caitilin Walsh
Copy Editors: Sue Barton, Nancy Boatwright, Diana Boyle
and Donnie Weigand

The author assumes full responsibility for any errors that
may remain in the text, as changes where made after they
had a chance to look things over.

Published by Magee Research
1075 Bellevue Way NE, #161
Bellevue, Washington 98004
Web Site: www.bdance.com/bdance
Email: mir@bdance.com

First Edition: June, 1996

Brain Dancing is a trademark of Magee Research.

Library of Congress Catalog Card Number: 96-094115

ISBN: 0-9646260-0-4

For Mom

"Captain, My Captain"

Just as music is beyond words because it is more precise, the love you have shared with me is beyond music.

CONTENTS

ACKNOWLEDGEMENTS

I am deeply grateful to the service men and women who risked their lives to create the freedom that made it possible for me to do the work and research required to write this book. I suspect that the toughest day at the office pales in comparison to the average day on the front line.

Brain Dancing was written while standing on the shoulders of intellectual giants who've gone before me. I am especially grateful to Richard Bandler, Tony Buzan, Stephen Covey, Anthony Robbins, and Peter Senge.

For the development and production of the book itself, I feel a deep sense of gratitude to:

* My brother and mentor, Mike.
* My uncle, Vernon Bowlby, who first introduced me to Nightengale-Conant audiotapes and taught me several important life lessons.
* My friend, Teresa Dahl, for directing me to so many excellent teachers, and for valuable collaboration that influenced several major themes in this book.
* The members of my Toastmasters club, Premier Presenters. Especially, Donnie, Sue, Jan, Jim, Amy D., Wayne, Cindy, Diane, Joe, Caron, Lina, Rita, Bruce, Amy L., Sally, Charlene, Deborah, Jeff, Dave, Elise, Steve H., Karen, Steve D., John, Dennis, David, Jerry, Audrey, Garth, Carolyn, Betsy, Tom, Julia, Dennis, and Mark. Also Karna, Stuart, Lida, Chuck and Paul from Eastside Toastmasters. Somehow we made miracles happen in those meetings, and my life will never be the same. Thank you for demonstrating a commitment to excellence that inspired me to do my best.

★ My friend and mentor, Irv Becker, for wise council which included the encouragement to join Toastmasters.

★ Caitilin Walsh, for her editing assistance.

★ My sister, Nancy, for her copy editing assistance.

★ Diana Boyle, for her copy editing assistance.

★ Professor Sailors and Professor Savey at Western Washington University, for your dedication to teaching excellence and wise council of such lasting value.

★ Professor Robert Killingstad at Everett Community College. You made learning calculus fun and helped ignite my interest in learning.

★ Judy Roberts at Mountlake Terrace High School. I remember feeling that you believed in my potential, even though there wasn't much to based it on, except that which can be seen by the most caring eyes.

★ The individuals at the companies who gave me their vote of confidence by selecting me to work on projects which allowed me to develop and test the ideas presented in this book. Thank you for the opportunity to be of service

PREFACE

We are about to enter a century where technical problem-solving skills will carry increasing influence for individuals, organizations and countries. In the spirit of the reengineering efforts being applied to business processes, Brain Dancing is the culmination of a 3½ year effort to optimize the mental processes involved in developing technical capacity. While implementing technology over the past 15 years, I've noticed certain mental processes get performed repeatedly. Processes such as directing our vast subconscious resources, managing the flow of ideas during discussions with teammates, creative problem solving, reading and remembering. To this end, I've examined the best understanding I could find on how our mind works, and used these ideas to formulate strategies that optimize these mental processes.

During a 1992 speech, Peter Senge quoted Mr. Matsushita, head of the Japanese industrial giant, as saying, "The West will not catch up." Mr. Matsushita based this belief on his observation that Western business leaders idea of management is getting ideas out of the heads of people at the top into the 'hands' of people at the bottom. "For us," he continued, "the essence of management, is the mobilization of the intellectual resources of everyone in the organization."[1]

Untapped intellectual resources represent the greatest underutilized resource of our nation. It is widely claimed that most people use less than 10% of their mental capacity. Brain Dancing is my attempt to embrace the possibility of mobilizing the remaining 90% within the context of a balanced lifestyle. If a substantial number of people use even

---

[1] This quote was included as part of Peter Senge's keynote address to the 1992 Goal/PC conference.

an additional 10% for an extended period of time, the resulting impact on society would be significant.

For some   people, this means taking on projects that challenge them in new ways—tipping the first domino. For the technical leaders such as those responsible for helping the U.S. bring microcomputer technology to the world, these ideas may help fine tune their mental strategies. For students about to enter the workforce, Brain Dancing is a chance to sharpen their mental toolset before getting swooped up by society's insatiable demand for technical capacity.

The term "Brain Dancing" originated out of my efforts to describe the mental synergy that results from mobilizing right-brain thought processes, especially in those individuals who habitually favor the left side. Right-brain creativity gives the left side more and better ideas to analyze. The disciplined structure of the left provides a framework for organizing these ideas and coming up with questions that stimulate additional creativity. The result is a dynamic loop between the two hemispheres—a "brain dance". As you will discover, this metaphor has evolved over the past 3 years to include additional oscillations that are not necessarily between left and right-brain thinking.

Working on technical projects for dozens of companies has been my laboratory for testing the usefulness of various self-development techniques. These projects include the Boeing 777, multi-million dollar real estate deals for Weyerhaeuser, and, over the last 30 months, software related projects with Microsoft.

My research included firewalks at Anthony Robbins' "Fear into Power" events, reading hundreds of self-development books, and investing hundreds of hours attending personal- development seminars and listening to audiotapes in my "university on wheels". Which techniques worked the best? How can they be learned and applied without disrupting technical momentum? Brain Dancing is my answer to these questions.

Brain Dancing was written for "knowledge workers". I define "knowledge worker" as anyone looking for a better way of doing something. Finding "a better way" requires new information and new thought—it involves using your brain to solve problems. Solving problems builds specialized skills, knowledge and self-confidence. These combine to increase your capacity for effective action, and thus position you to take on similar projects of increasing complexity. I use the term "project" to refer to a chunk of work with a definite ending that you can focus on. Projects are the fundamental building block of specialized technical capacity. As explained in Chapter 2, everything starts when you take on a project that gives you a reason to think in new ways and learn new material.

An ad in the Wall Street Journal in the mid-eighties showed the head of Greek statue. Its nose had either fallen off or been broken off. The caption read: "Sometimes when you keep your nose to the grindstone, all you get is a flat nose." In the words of Dr. W. Edwards Deming: "Let's not talk about working harder. Everyone is already working their hardest. Work smarter." I hope the information that follows will help you work smarter by optimizing strategic mental processes performed frequently in your work. We are all doing the best we can. The key is to learn how to improve what our "best" is.

Patrick Magee
Bellevue, Washington

CHAPTER 1

MENTAL LEVERAGE

"Only as far as we seek can we go...Only as much as we dream can we become."

— Anonymous

→ A large ocean liner traveling at 15 knots would require several tons of force on the bow to make it turn. Instead, a rudder is used, which swings the back end around, causing the ship to turn. The rudder on an ocean liner is so large however, that tremendous force is required to turn it as well. So the technique is applied again by placing a trim tab on the rudder—a rudder's rudder. When the helmsman turns the wheel, it turns the trim tab, which turns the rudder, which turns the ship. In this way a small action properly focused can have a significant impact on the overall direction of the ship—the overall system.[2]

My goal with *Brain Dancing* is to present you with ideas that offer the potential for "mental leverage". Ideas that offer the highest potential return per minute of learning time invested.

As summarized in Figure 1.1, many great thinkers have emphasized the importance of our thoughts. The purpose of my research has been to discover exactly what I can do differently upon arriving at the office to take maximum advantage of this great truth.

---

[2] Adapted from ideas presented by Peter Senge in his book, *The Fifth Discipline*.

"The greatest discovery of my generation is that a human being can alter his life by altering his attitude of mind." William James.

"I know of no more encouraging fact than the unquestionable ability of man to elevate his life by conscious endeavor." Henry David Thoreau

"For as he thinketh in his heart, so he is." Proverbs 23:7

"A man is what he thinks about all day long." Ralph Waldo Emerson

"Change your thoughts and you change your world...You are not what you think you are; but what you think, you are." Norman Vincent Peale

"If you think you can or if you think you can't, you're right." Henry Ford

"The thought is the ancestor of the deed." Thomas Carlyle

"You become what you think about." Earl Nightengale

"Our life is what our thoughts make it." Marcus Aurelius Antoninus

"Sow a thought, reap an action, sow an action, reap a habit, sow a habit, reap a character, sow a character, reap a destiny." Anonymous

"Go thy way, and as thou hast believed, so be it done unto thee." Matthew 8:13

"All that man achieves is the direct result of his own thoughts...A man can only rise, conquer and achieve by lifting up his thoughts." James Allen

Figure 1.1. Quotes on the Importance of Thought.

Scale	Range of Thought
Focus	Daydreaming↔Concentrated Focus
Awareness	Subconscious←————→Conscious
Time Orientation	Past←———→Present←———→Future
Decision	Minor←————————→Destiny Shaping
Question	Questions←————————→Answers
Modality	Kinesthetic←→Auditory←—→Visual
Attitude	Positive←————————→Negative
Emotion	Passionate←————————→Ambivalent
Brain Wave Frequency	Delta←—→Theta←—→Alpha←—→Beta
Dialogue	None←————————→Many People
Detail Level	General←————————→Specific

Figure 1.2. Thought Spectrum Chart.

→ My research uncovered a variety of thought types summarized in Figure 1.2. The question then became, "Which thoughts?"

abcdefghijklmnopqrstuvwxyz

If hundreds of thousands of words in the English language can be derived from just 26 letters, then imagine how many different kinds of thoughts there must be. How is a person supposed to coordinate the mental dance between all these types of thought?

Oftentimes, it was difficult to do all the things the authors suggested and still get my work done. There was a growing discrepancy between what I was learning and what I was doing. Admittedly, some of this was due to the fact that I was not working on problems that required the application of what they taught.

"For men are wiser than they know," wrote Emerson. We often dance in and out of these various thought categories effortlessly, or unawares, as we go through our daily routines. We do not need a label for something in order to do it. Some of these thought types are worthy of conscious intervention, however, which leads us to...

DECISIONS: THE FULCRUM OF MENTAL EFFECTIVENESS

➤   Using willpower, you can decide to think any of the thoughts in the above spectrum at any given moment. You can decide to have faith, to be happy, to go into an alpha wave state, to ask questions or think of answers, to think in pictures, words or feelings, to think about what has already occurred, the present or the future, to concentrate or to daydream. You decide whether to think about an issue alone or discuss it with others. Each moment offers infinite choices. Yet it takes energy and mental resources to make decisions, and the threat of decisional stress increases as infoglut expands and our choices multiply.

Consider the words of Peter Drucker from *The Effective Executive*: "Effective Executives do not make a great many decisions. They concentrate on the important ones. They try to think through what is strategic and generic, rather than 'solve problems.' They try to make a few important decisions on the highest level of conceptual understanding."

The process of making "a few important decisions" is to move up the scale as in Figure 1.4. This shifts the fulcrum to the left in Figure 1.5, making it easier to lift the weight. For example, writing this book required thousands of decisions. The most important decisions occurred at the top of the hierarchy, which "cascaded down" to the lower levels. It was far more important that I got the top-level decisions correct.

This is a fairly simple and obvious distinction with which to begin my book. Yet every chapter rests squarely on the notion of traversing levels of thought to focus upon what is "strategic and generic" in our thinking processes.

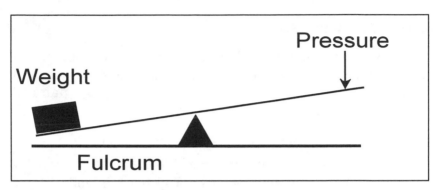

Figure 1.3. Fulcrum Metaphor.

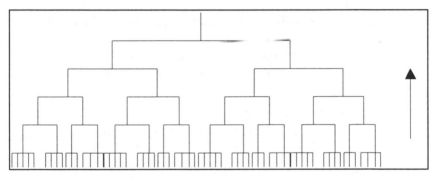

Figure 1.4. Layers of "Conceptual Understanding" at which decisions can be made.

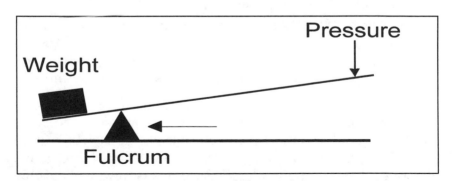

Figure 1.5. Fulcrum shifts to left when energies focused on effective high level decisions.

CHAPTER OVERVIEWS

→   The overriding theme of Brain Dancing is to manage the mental dance between complementary opposite modes of thinking. Chapters 2 through 6 describe four pairs of complementary opposites:

Conscious ←——→ Subconscious
Individual Thought ←——→ Dialogue
Left-Brain Mode ←——→ Right-Brain Mode
Detailed Thought ←——→ High Level Thought

- **Chapters 2 and 3**: The interplay between conscious and subconscious mental processes. The key to mobilizing our vast subconscious mental resources is learning to direct our brains with effective self-communication.
- **Chapter 4**: Thinking alone vs. engaging in dialogue. Something special happens to our thinking whenever two or more people discuss an issue they care about.
- **Chapter 5**: Right-brain vs. left-brain thinking modes. Each brain hemisphere is specialized, and mental leverage can be obtained by overcoming the common tendency to favor one side.
- **Chapter 6**: Detailed vs. "big picture" thinking. Just as information has structure, so do our thoughts. At the highest level, there are processes we use to perform key mental processes, and these processes can be optimized.

These chapters lay down the foundation of the Brain Dancing strategy. Each chapter presents you with two types of information: 1) underlying principles; and 2) what to do differently based on these distinctions. Chapter 7 then describes how I apply all of these ideas toward learning software faster, which is becoming an increasingly high leverage use of our time. It takes energy to apply these ideas, so Chapter 8 discusses my favorite strategies for increasing personal energy. And lastly, Chapter 9 describes some lessons personal energy. And lastly, Chapter 9 describes some lessons I've learned about maintaining balance as you strive to mobilize untapped intellectual resources.

Each chapter focuses on high level strategic decisions I use to work smarter, learn faster, and manage information more effectively.

WE ARE "IN-FORMATION"

➔   Deepak Chopra makes the observation that we are literally "information"—pronounced in-formation. Information has an impact on our decisions, decisions affect our actions, actions affect our habits, our habits determine our character, and our character determines our destiny. We are "information" because better information helps us make better decisions.

An extreme example of this occurred when I was 12. My father died suddenly and unexpectedly of a heart attack at the age of 49. Dad died, at least in part, because we lacked the information that could have saved him: that his arteries were blocked by arteriosclerosis. This information could have led to some decisions that might have made a difference. I have no way of knowing for sure how much the "hand of fate" had to do with this.

Information literally shapes my life in countless ways: what and how I eat, when and how I exercise, how I carry myself, smile, think, communicate, etc. The most powerful information is "MetaInformation"—information that improves the processes we use to interact with information—which is what this book is about.

A WORD ON PERSONAL ECOLOGY

Your subconscious mind does a lot of remarkable things for you. One of its responsibilities is self-preservation. If you learn a technique that increases your personal power, and you do not have the discipline or strength of character to direct that increased power in disciplined ways, then using that technique could actually prove harmful to you. Fortunately, in most cases the subconscious mind has a clever way of filtering ideas out of our "awareness" when we are not ready for them.

For this reason, I encourage you to study the work of Stephen Covey (*7 Habits, First Things First*) and Scott Peck (*The Road Less Traveled*) in conjunction with this text. These books deal with the issue of character development and are written so brilliantly it often boggles my mind to read them. They give specific instructions on how to build the mental and physical infrastructure that makes the learning and application of *Brain Dancing* techniques "ecological".

Computer industry analyst Esther Dyson touched on this phenomenon when she said, "People who succeed in the computer industry tend to accumulate more and more power until they implode." You may already be beyond the need for these books, but I can tell you first hand that I've "imploded" a few times and it was not fun. Chapter 9 addresses this issue in depth.

POWERFUL QUESTIONS

→ It has been said that when one is truly ready for something, it will put in its appearance. This is similar to the Chinese proverb, "When a student is ready, a teacher appears." Ever wonder what a person can do to increase the rate at which they are ready for new growth and learning?

> *"A powerful question can be vastly more useful than any answer."*
>
> *— Peter Senge*

CHAPTER 2

THE SOLUTIONS APPROACH TO CAPACITY ENHANCEMENT

"Capacities clamor to be used and cease their clamor only when they are well used."

—— Abraham Maslow

"People don't see the world as it is. They see it as they are."

—— Stephen Covey

→   In the movie *Apollo 13*, the actor playing Jim Lovell states, "It wasn't a miracle that we went to the moon. We just decided to go." This decision created a context in which information about going to the moon could be applied. The information was always there waiting to be discovered, we just needed a reason to discover it.

Woven into this experience is a basic truth with broad application. If you want to use more of your brain, if you want to increase your understanding of something, then give yourself a reason to do so. A reason such as solving a problem or teaching others a better way of doing something. The following chapters present you with hundreds of ideas. Your interaction with and understanding of these ideas, will depend upon the context you create in which to apply them.

We have been encouraged to set goals and to "begin with the end in mind." The reason this is great advice is related to the first set of complementary opposites I'll address—conscious and subconscious thinking.

It is often suggested that most people use less than 10% of their mental capacity. Just for kicks, ask someone if they feel they are using less than 10% of their brain. If they say yes, ask them to use 100% just for a moment. Tell them you are just curious what difference it would make. Seriously, what *does* it mean to use less than 10%?

→ Consider the diagram in Figure 2.1. The large circle represents the mental capacity of the subconscious mind, and the small dot the relative capacity of the conscious mind. The diagram is actually wrong because the dot representing the conscious mind is far too big! Milton

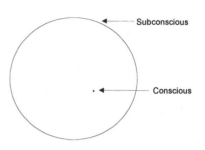

Figure 2.1

Erickson, the greatest hypnotherapist ever, said, "The conscious mind is brilliant and the unconscious mind is a hell of a lot smarter."

If it is true that someone is using less than 10% of their mental capacity, then what part of their mind are they most likely underutilizing? The above diagram suggests that over 99% of our mental capacity is subconscious, which means that people are underutilizing their subconscious minds.

The "subconscious mind" is defined as everything that is going on in your mind that you are not aware of. The brain/mind is so complex, it is difficult to find words to describe it that don't fall short to some degree. I use the term "subconscious" because it provides a useful way of describing events in a context that helps people run their mind more effectively.

How does a person mobilize underutilized intellectual resources? This entire book is my full answer to this question. A good place to begin is to take on a project or set a goal that demands it of you. After investing 25 years writing *The Story of Civilization*, Will Durant concluded, "Not to think unless we have to—there is much to be said for this as the summation of wisdom." Committing to do a project that stretches your capacities puts you in a position where you "have to".

"You are much bigger, brighter, stronger, healthier— you've got more energy and more power than you are ever going to discover until you have to."

— Anthony Robbins

→   Have you ever awoken in the middle of the night and "noticed" that your mind was cranking away on a work related issue? That was your subconscious running on automatic pilot. If you have ever driven a car and carried on a conversation, then you were relying on subconscious mental processes to handle most of the driving. Here's a simple experiment: Pick up a paper clip or some other small object, toss it up in the air about a foot and then catch it. Were you consciously directing each muscle when you did this? That was a pretty complex act from a neuro-physiological point of view, when you consider that subconscious mental processes were directing muscular activity in your shoulder, arm, and hand. Your conscious mind focused on the "what" - catch object, and your subconscious took care of the details - contract nerves x, y and z, increase flow of blood to shoulder arm and hand, etc.

Your subconscious mind is doing similarly complex tasks with every action you take, whether it be typing a report, delivering a speech, or communicating with an associate. Your subconscious is an obedient and able servant once it knows which direction you want to go, what outcome you want to achieve. Self-communication is the process of directing your subconscious mind, and you know you are "self-communicating" effectively when your actions are moving you closer to your desired outcome.

I once heard a story of a photographer whose actions demonstrated an understanding of this principle, even though the story was told to make a different point. This photographer wanted to take a small number of photographs that depicted the essence of an unusual Indian horse race. Upon arriving at the scene, rather than just starting to take pictures, he spent a day surveying the situation. That evening, he listed the journalistic points he wanted to make, and the images that must appear in the pictures to accurately represent this culture. Then he imagined potential photographs which would contain as many of these elements as possible. He wanted to take photos that would do double or triple-duty, so that the reader would see a rather small set of photos that said it all. Over the next few days, he began taking photographs while keeping these images in his mind. While doing this, he remained completely open to whatever he might find along the way, including new dimensions to the story he'd missed on the first day. He didn't get all of the points or all of the photographs, but he got a lot of them. He also took and used photographs that he hadn't imagined.

In my opinion, this photographer's strategy demonstrated a keen understanding of how to manage the interaction between conscious and subconscious thinking. By investing the time up front imagining photographs that might address multiple aspects of the culture, he had consciously primed his subconscious mind—the seat of action—to be on the lookout for specific combinations of circumstances, and his actions were directed accordingly.

After consciously deciding to take on a challenging project, the next thing you need to do is inform your subconscious mind. "Hey, excuse me, uh-hum!" While our conscious mind dances and darts, the subconscious mind operates more like a giant steamship. According to Paul Harvey, steamship captains navigate by looking a mile down river. They know that these large boats will continue on their present course long after they have turned the wheel. Similarly, our subconscious mind guides our actions in ways that move us in a specified direction. There is often so much mental chitchat going on, that special measures are required to let the subconscious know when to pay attention. Most of Chapter 3 focuses on specific strategies for "self-communicating" your desired direction to your subconscious mind.

THE ULTIMATE INFORMATION FILTER

➔   In addition to guiding our actions, subconscious mental processes also heavily influence what information catches our attention. Have you ever purchased a new car and then begun to "notice" similar cars everywhere you drive? That was your subconscious filtering information into your awareness based on what it thought you might like to know.

Deciding to complete a project forms the basis for filtering the blizzard of information being generated by our increasingly complex society. Consider the words of Aldous Huxley from his book, *The Doors of Perception*: "The suggestion is that the function of the brain and nervous system and sense organs is in the main eliminative and not productive. Each person is at each moment capable of remembering all that has ever happened to him and of perceiving everything that is happening everywhere in the universe. The function of the brain and nervous system is to protect us from being overwhelmed and confused by this mass of largely useless and irrelevant knowledge, by shutting out most of what we should otherwise perceive or remember at any moment, and leaving only that very small and special selection which is likely to be practically useful."

When you self-communicate a clearly defined outcome to your subconscious, it will use this directional guidance to filter relevant information into your awareness. This situation is analogous to the process our bodies use to build DNA strands. A small particle or enzyme sits at the junction of two strands. Its job is to grab particles that float by and use them to build what ends up looking like a spiral staircase. It somehow "knows" which particles to grab from the thousands that drift by—particles that fit perfectly into the next open spot. In the same way, our subconscious mind sifts the vast quantities of information that drift by our awareness. When a clear outcome has been defined and communicated, it is easier for the subconscious to recognize useful information that it should "present to our awareness".

When considering a potential project, the most important question I ask the project organizer is:

> At the end of this project, how will you know that I did an outstanding job?

I am asking for the evidence procedure this person will use to evaluate my performance. It tells me how clearly the boundary conditions for the project have been determined. Without this clarity, I end up with a "creeping request", where I am unable to clearly communicate direction to my subconscious because the direction is constantly changing. The situation is analogous to having your manager standing over your bowling lane blocking your view with a sheet. You throw the ball, and your manager tells you how many pins you knocked down. More importantly, if the project outcome has not been clearly defined, you don't even know which lane to use.

As I begin my fifth project at Microsoft, literally thousands of pages of reading material pile up before me. In addition, people around me are generating volumes of related information as they work. "Two things seemed pretty apparent to me," wrote Mark Twain, "One was, that in order to be a [Mississippi River] pilot a man had got to learn more than any one man ought to be allowed to know; and the other was, that he must learn it all over again in a different way every 24 hours."

As I "pilot" my way through this information maze, I am comforted by the fact that only a small fraction of this information is directly applicable to the work I must complete. The challenge is determining which one to ten percent to focus on. By investing in clarity up front, and "self-communicating" a clear picture of the desired end result to my subconscious mind, I am programming its information filtering mechanisms to guide my actions and awareness.

Somehow, as I'm flipping through the pages, or having conversations with associates, my subconscious directs me to the information I need. The information filtering capacity of the subconscious mind is quite miraculous. Every project I've ever worked on has offered increasing evidence of the truly amazing power of this principle. There is much evidence that a belief in this process can influence the degree to which it is true for you.

Perhaps our educational system could use this distinction to balance book learning with learning in which the intended outcome is useful action, as opposed to completing a written test.

USING PROJECTS FOR CAPACITY ENHANCEMENT

→   What exactly is a project? I use the term to describe a chunk of work with a clear ending. It may be creating a new product, implementing a new system, or creating a spreadsheet to help optimize a business process.

When you commit to do a project, problems arise. In solving these problems you accomplish three things:

- You acquire specialized knowledge about solving these types of problems
- You develop specialized skills useful in solving these types of problems
- You increase your self-confidence in your ability to solve these types of problems

These three factors combine to increase your capacity to complete similar projects. My experience suggests that nature abhors unused capacity. This increased capacity tends to draw into your awareness opportunities to solve similar problems of increasing complexity. In this way, the problems you choose to solve will take you in a direction and can thus be destiny shaping. In the words of Nobel Prize laureate Albert Szent-Gyorgyi, "Ability brings with it the need to use that ability."

What a person desires to do is influenced by their existing capacity. This perspective was inspired by Emerson's statement: "There is nothing capricious in nature, and the implanting of a desire indicates that its gratification is in the constitution of the creature who feels it." A person is not likely to have a burning desire to do something beyond their ability. If, through the completion of a series of projects of increasing complexity, you enhance your capacity in a certain area, you can indirectly impact what you desire.

"We operate in an economy that rewards specialization."

— *Bill Gates*

RIVER OF INCREASING SWIFTNESS

→   I started my career in public accounting. One day it dawned on me that at any moment, the Government could come along and pull the rug out from all my hard work, by totally rearranging the tax laws I was working so hard to master. Switching fields to computer programming has not exactly been a safe haven from change. Beginning in 1982, I invested twelve months learning to program in COBOL and haven't used COBOL since. During the mid-80's I became proficient in four other non-Windows programming languages. I haven't used any of these languages for over three years. Over the last four years I've learned three Windows-based programming languages, any one of which is larger in scope than the four DOS-based languages combined! To top it off, I'm now beginning to learn a programming technology whose scope easily exceeds the material in the previous three Windows programming languages combined!

From my perspective, information is flowing through society like a river of increasing swiftness. It seems to be getting less important to be able to master the complete content of this river at any given moment, and more important to be able to interact with this river as it relates to your current project. Paul Zane Pilzer hit the nail right on the head when he said,

"People who learn things the fastest will do much better than those who learn things the best." In an environment of rapid change, the ability to learn quickly may be the ultimate competitive advantage. Interacting with this "information river" means being able to quickly locate and use information related to completing the current project. Using your subconscious information filtering capacity is a great strategy for doing this.

DAILY SAW SHARPENING

→ If you make projects your only source of specialized knowledge, you risk substantially limiting your career. The complementary opposite of highly-focused project learning is to invest at least one hour per day doing general non-project research in your field of study. When working on a project, pay particular attention to information related to that project as discussed above. During this hour, however, I suggest that you forget about the project, and study topics related to your field that interest you. I am often amazed at how the two eventually overlap—that which I learn while doing non-project research often plays a significant role in future projects.

> *"Specialized knowledge is the basis of all value added."*
>
> *— Tom Peters*

Sticking to this one hour a day (or some other fixed time limit) is critical for this non-project research. In this case, there is no customer with a clearly defined need to serve as a feedback loop on your progress. It is thus easy to lose track of time. You work on projects until they have been completed, you do non-project research only until the time limit is up.

I agree with Earl Nightingale's statement that if you consistently devote one hour per day accumulating specialized knowledge in your field, then in five years, you will be a recognized leader in that field. Knowledge seems to compound much like interest in a savings account.

CATCHING A TECHNOLOGY WAVE—GETTING STARTED

Acquiring specialized capacity is a Catch-22. Getting the opportunity to work on projects is where most specialized capacity is acquired. Yet it is often difficult to get a company to hire you for such projects until after you've acquired related experience. With the pace of technological change accelerating, an increasing number of opportunities are being created to solve problems which have never been solved before. Additionally, I agree with Paul Zane Pilzer when he writes in *Unlimited Wealth*, that the technology gap—the difference between the best technology available and that actually in use—is greater today than at any time in our history.

"Focused action beats brilliance any day."

— Art Turock

In retrospect, the best strategy I see is to get a technical degree at the best learning institution available to you. Use this degree as a stepping stone into a position at an established company in order to learn the ropes of that industry. However, this book was written for people already in the workforce, so here are some things to consider:

1) "The value of information is in direct proportion to the number of people who know it," according to Harvey McKay. If you start out to learn a new technology and it proves difficult, consider adopting the attitude that this is a good sign. The rewards arel likely be higher because these barriers will keep out the weak of heart.

➜ 2) Align new projects with existing specialized capacity. Take on projects that require a combination of what you already know and new technology. Technology is moving so rapidly that it is often difficult for schools to keep up to date. Incrementally transitioning yourself into new fields allows you to use this cutting edge factor to your advantage. By choosing projects in new areas that leverage off existing skills and knowledge, you reduce the risk of biting off more than you can chew.

3) Consider correspondence school options. Open University in England has been a great success. In addition, the Internet is expanding the opportunities for distance learning.

4) Consider participating in on-line communities and solving the problems that people bring up there. CompuServe forums, Internet news groups and mailing lists provide such opportunities.

5) Build products that demonstrate what you know. I've always liked the saying: "When your work speaks for itself, don't interrupt." I used this approach in 1984 and as a result, was hired by Paul Brainerd to create the financial model he used in Aldus Corporation's early business plans.

6) Start or participate in trade associations such as user groups, or create some other opportunity to teach that which you want to master. The "authority figure" approach works if you chunk things down. Give presentations on narrow aspects of the field until you've covered enough of them to build some momentum with the technology. While this may sound contradictory, my experience has been that something special happens to our awareness when we definitely commit to a project or presentation. When you give yourself a reason to understand the material, it will make itself available to you.

7) Anticipate technology shifts. For example, right now there are an incredible number of entrepreneurial opportunities related to the Internet. New opportunities exist at almost every company for applying this budding communications capacity in innovative ways.

"Any man is educated who knows where to get knowledge when he needs it, and how to organize that knowledge into definite plans of action."

— *Napoleon Hill*

CONCLUSION

Conscious ←——→ Subconscious
Individual Thought ←——→ Dialogue
Left-Brain Mode ←——→ Right-Brain Mode
Detailed Thought ←——→ High Level Thought

This chapter introduced the first major pair of complementary opposite modes of thinking – managing the interplay between conscious and subconscious thought. After consciously selecting a goal or project, invest in clarifying the outcome. Then consciously self-communicate that specific outcome to your subconscious information filtering action guidance mechanisms, which leads us to Chapter 3.

"I don't care who you are.
I don't care where you come from.
I don't care where you went to school.
I don't care if you went to school.
I don't care what race you are.
I don't care what color you are.
I don't care what religion you are.
I care about what you can do and what you've done lately."

— *Ross Perot*

CHAPTER 3

HIGH BANDWIDTH
SELF-COMMUNICATION

"Brains don't learn to get results; they learn to go in directions."

— *Richard Bandler*

"It's not what the vision is, it's what the vision does."

— *Alan Kay*

Your subconscious is an obedient and able servant once it knows which direction you want to go. Self-communication is the process of directing your subconscious mind, and you know you are self-communicating effectively when your actions are moving you closer to your desired outcome.

As explained in Chapter 2, the vast majority of our mental capacity resides in the subconscious. People using less than ten percent of their brain are probably underutilizing this part of their mind. Some self-communication techniques are more effective than others, employing skills useful in many other contexts. For these reasons, the strategies presented in this chapter are excellent opportunities to achieve mental leverage.

This chapter begins with a review of the basic principles of self-communication. The following four strategies for high bandwidth self-communication are then explained:

1) Pumping Ions - Developing your "visualization muscle". Four exercises are presented (mental snapshot, submodality, drawing, and ten minute visualization) to help you develop this skill.
2) Using metaphors to communicate meaning both to others and to your subconscious at higher bandwidths.
3) Full physiology affirmations involve thinking about your desired outcomes at moments when you have developed powerful physiologies.
4) Employing alpha brain waves by thinking about your desired outcome in a state of relaxed alertness.

Self-communication is a two-way street. The above strategies sow the seeds, yet you must also develop the ability to "tune-in" to intuitive guidance as it blossoms from your subconscious mind. Thus I conclude the chapter with a brief discussion of intuition.

PRINCIPLES

The principles of self-communication are:

1) There are two dimensions to self-communication: physical and mental.
2) When you truly understand and believe in the power of your subconscious, you won't hesitate to use high bandwidth self-communication techniques daily. You may even look forward to it.
3) Give yourself a reason to use the untapped mental capacity of your subconscious mind.
4) Your mind cannot focus on the opposite of an idea.
5) Your subconscious continues to process or "incubate" issues even when you are not consciously thinking about them.
6) The effectiveness of your self-communication is diminished to the extent it contradicts existing beliefs or behavior patterns that your subconscious mind

believes are important to you. Your desired direction must be personally ecological.

7) A picture is worth a thousand words in your mind as well.

PRINCIPLE #1: THE TWO DIMENSIONS OF SELF-COMMUNICATION

The way you use your physiology has a direct impact on how you feel. To quote William James: "Action seems to follow feeling, but really action and feeling go together; and by regulating the action, which is under the more direct control of the will, we can indirectly regulate the feeling, which is not."

In this sense, your physiology is a key part of self-communication. The section on affirmations later in this chapter describes how to combine this distinction with "mental" forms of self-communication for increased effectiveness. One of the basic challenges of self-communication is helping the subconscious cut through all the mental noise. If our subconscious mind didn't have some means of distinguishing true directional communication from mental chit-chat, our actions might be somewhat erratic. When you combine congruent physiology with emotionally charged affirmations, it says to your subconscious, "Pay attention!"

PRINCIPLE #2: BELIEVE IN THE POWER OF YOUR SUBCONSCIOUS

If you truly believe in the awesome potential of directing your subconscious, you wouldn't hesitate to apply self-communication techniques such as visualization. There is so much evidence that they work, that it is no longer a question of *if* they work, it is only a question of *when*. The answer is that self-communication works when you have figured out how to do the right processes in your mind.

→   According to Richard Bandler and John Grinder, co-developers of Neuro Linguistic Programming (NLP), "The meaning of your communication is the response you get." I believe this applies to both interpersonal and intrapersonal communication (i.e., thought). We do not have the ability to transfer mental software from one brain to another in the same way we transfer computer software today. You can't hand someone a disk and say, "Here, load this into your brain and give it a try." Consequently, one of the best ways to tell if you are truly running the same mental software as someone else is by the results you are getting. Your feedback loop is the direction your actions are taking you. If at the end of a day, week or month, you can look back on your actions and see they are taking you in the direction you want to go, then to that extent, you are self-communicating effectively. To quote Richard Bandler, "Brains, like computers, are not 'user-friendly.' They do exactly what they're told to do, not what you want them to do."

When you consider how many decisions went into the writing of *Brain Dancing*, you'll understand why I believe that the quality of this book is in direct proportion to the degree to which I have successfully communicated my desired outcome to my subconscious. It's not what the vision is, but what it does. That's how you know if you are self-communicating effectively.

PRINCIPLE #3: GIVE YOURSELF A REASON TO USE YOUR SUBCONSCIOUS

Consider what would happen if the electric company suddenly sent twice as much power down the lines to your city. Would the PC on your desk suddenly run twice as fast? Would your dishwasher do its cycles in less time? That's not how it works. The extra power would be wasted.

Nature despises waste, and your subconscious is a mental power reserve. The valve that opens the channel is this: you must give yourself a reason to use this mental power. In his book, *The Power of Your Subconscious Mind*, Dr. Joseph

Murphy tells the story of a young man who asked Socrates how he could obtain wisdom. Socrates took the lad to a river, pushed the boy's head under the water, and held it there until the boy was gasping for air. He then relaxed and released his head. When the boy regained his composure, he asked him what he desired most while under water.

"I wanted air," said the boy.

Socrates replied, "When you want wisdom as much as you wanted air when you were immersed in the water, you will receive it."

Having a problem to solve, somebody to help, something to create, or something to teach to another—and wanting to do it as badly as that boy wanted air—that's what opens the flood gates of your subconscious mental power.

PRINCIPLE #4: YOUR MIND CANNOT FOCUS ON THE OPPOSITE OF AN IDEA

➔ It is better to say to someone "Drive safely" than to say, "Don't crash." Your mind moves in directions. Doesn't it make sense that telling your mind where you want to go is more precise than telling it where not to go? There is also the argument that each time you think a thought you increase the likelihood of bringing it into existence. In order to "not" think something you have to first "think" of the thing you're not supposed to think about. This principle is referred to in several books and also seems to jibe with my intuition.

Wayne Dyer offers a corollary to this: "Everything you are *for* strengthens you, and everything you are *against* weakens you." Invest your mental energy into things you want to encourage. That gives you two choices: positive mental energy and neutral (i.e., no mental energy).

What you pay attention to determines what you get.
What you pay attention to determines what you miss.

— Anonymous

PRINCIPLE #5: INCUBATION

➔   If you have ever awoken in the middle of the night and noticed that your mind was "processing" a work related issue, then you understand what I'm referring to as "incubation". The subconscious mind seems to run on automatic pilot while we are off doing other things. My experience suggests that incubation occurs at a variety of levels on a variety of issues over time. I have no way of knowing whether my subconscious is working on multiple issues simultaneously or just doing a little here and there. For example, sometimes I'll listen to an educational audiotape series several times and feel overwhelmed by the material. Listening to the same tapes one year later often reveals that I've actually been applying some of the things which seemed confusing to me a year ago. In the words of William James, "We learn to swim in winter and skate in summer."

In his excellent book, *The Intuitive Edge*, Philip Goldberg writes that this "nonconscious synthesis" occurs while we are sleeping, walking in nature, or doing our chores. In his words, "The factory of the mind continues to work while the manager is out, assembling diverse raw materials and putting them together in unusual ways to create new products."

You can apply this distinction any time you anticipate a need to learn a new skill or topic for a project. Get your subconscious working in this new area as soon as possible. In some cases, you can begin this incubation process by taking just five minutes twice a week to do a high level scan of the material—at least until your schedule permits more in depth study.

If you are learning a new skill, begin doing the activity a couple of times a week for just five minutes. For example, in anticipation of the need to create audiotapes of this book, I did a couple of five-minute recording sessions at home using an inexpensive portable tape recorder. I did this several weeks in advance of actually needing to use the skill to get my mind/body accustomed to going through the new set of actions.

Incubation is one reason why it is often so helpful to finish each day by reviewing priorities for the next. Prime your mind for action when you arrive the next morning. In her superb autobiography, Mary Kay Ash (of Mary Kay Cosmetics) writes that one key to her success has been her habit of taking a few moments at the end of each day to write down the six most important things she must accomplish the following day.

If writing a list doesn't work for you, consider using a more right-brain approach, such as drawing a mindmap (discussed in Chapter 5) as you visualize the following day going perfectly.

PRINCIPLE #6: PERSONAL ECOLOGY

One of the Neuro Linguistic Programming (NLP) techniques developed by Bandler and Grinder is called the "six-step reframe". This is a process where another person helps you establish a direct communication channel with your subconscious for the purpose of changing an unwanted behavior pattern. Your subconscious mind is asked to come up with three alternative behavior patterns. The final step involves asking your subconscious, "is there any part of me that objects to any of the three new alternatives?"

One time a friend was guiding me through a six-step reframe to help me stop picking at my fingernails. When she asked me this last question to do an "ecology check," my entire body started trembling and I had no idea why! This experience made it absolutely clear to me how important it is that our "self-communication" not contradict existing beliefs or behavior patterns that our subconscious believes are important to us.

For more information on the six-step reframe, refer to Anthony Robbins' book, *Unlimited Power* or Bandler and Grinder's book, *Reframing*.

PRINCIPLE #7: A PICTURE IS WORTH 1000 WORDS IN YOUR MIND AS WELL

→   Take a moment and "think" the following sentence:

"The dog jumped over the fence."

Now think the following picture:

Which thought was more efficient? To the degree that you can think the above picture almost instantaneously, you understand why mental pictures allow us to think at higher bandwidths. Most people can hold between five and nine ideas in their mind simultaneously. If pictures can be enriched to contain many objects or symbols and each symbol can represent multiple ideas, then this distinction can be used to break this 5-9 idea limitation.

Could Einstein have developed his theory of relativity without the ability to visualize himself hitching a ride on a beam of light emanating from the face of the clock? Nikola Tesla invented electrical generators by creating a mental image of the device and then running it for hours in his mind to see if his design would work.

Personally, the most useful aspect of thinking visually is that it allows me to traverse a series of related pictures much faster than I could describe the same thoughts with "mental words". If you have ever worked on a computer that used a character-based operating system such as DOS, and then switched to a graphical user interface such as Windows, then you understand the potential power of using a more visual approach to running your brain.

The remainder of this chapter discusses what you can do differently to align your actions with the above principles.

Pumping Ions: Developing Your Visualization Muscle

→ Your brain has something like a mental muscle that allows you to create and manipulate visual images. When you perform exercises that increase your ability to visualize, you are developing a mental capacity that can:

- Improve your ability to communicate with your subconscious mind: a picture is worth a thousand words in your mind as well.

- Increase your reading speed: the famous Evelyn Wood Reading Dynamics course is based on a "visual vertical" strategy (Chapter 6).

- Improve your memory: several memory training programs are based on the ability to quickly create outrageous, colorful, action-oriented pictures in your mind (Chapter 6).

- Increase your ability to think synergistically: visualizing mobilizes right-brain mental processes (Chapter 5).

- Allow yourself to think consciously at higher bandwidths: it is much more efficient to think a series of pictures than to say the words that the pictures represent.

Developing your mental visualization muscle is the "trim tab" or "rudder's rudder" of your mind, because concentrating on the development of this mental skill has the potential to impact multiple thought processes. When I did the visualization exercises in Kevin Trudeau's *Mega Memory* audiotape program, it wasn't clear how I was going to apply these techniques at work. While I don't use peg lists or picture stories on a daily basis, I do think more visually now than before. For example, when designing a user interface, rather than thinking in words, I now think in "screens" more proficiently. I see the mouse pointer clicking a button and the

next screen popping up. Instead of talking about these
screens in my mind's ear, I am seeing them in my mind's eye.
I can traverse a series of mental screens much faster than I
can "think" the paragraphs of words required to describe
them.

The processional benefits of developing my visualization
muscle did not end there. In studying Evelyn Wood's reading
program, I learned that a fundamental strategy for
increasing reading speed is to silence subvocalization by
"trusting my eyes" and thus reading visually. My mental
reading process went from:

see→say→understand

to just:

see→understand

Building up my visualization muscle helped me do this more
effectively. Admittedly, there are times when I still catch
myself subvocalizing. Sometimes I want to read slowly, such
as when reading conceptually dense material that is new.
However, when I want to scan a lot of material very quickly, I
am now able to cover more text in less time with greater
efficiency. Developing my "visualization muscle" plays a key
role in helping me become a more flexible reader.

My memory seemed to improve even if I wasn't using the
techniques. It became easier to take "mental snapshots" of
images and to convert ideas I am thinking or reading about
into pictures or symbols.

For knowledge workers, perhaps the highest leverage use of
this visualization muscle is for beginning projects with the
end in mind. Not all visualizations are created equal, and the
best visualizations are the ones that generate the most
effective actions toward project completion. If at the end of
each day, you can reflect on the day's activities and honestly
detect progress toward your goal, then you are on the right
track. Over time, through additional trial and error, you may

find that you can refine your visualizations to further enhance their effectiveness.

"The results you create depend on your clarity."

— Norm Levy

Some people are better at this than others, however. I know that this is a skill a person can develop because I used to be lousy at visualizing. The following four exercises have been helpful in developing my visualization muscle.

Before continuing, I must emphasize that you should not do these exercises if you are prone to extreme mood swings or have problems with depression. See Chapter 9 for details.

VISUALIZATION EXERCISE #1: MENTAL SNAPSHOT

Any time you have a free minute AND it is safe to briefly close your eyes, look at a nearby object, close your eyes, and notice if you can see the image in your "mind's eye". If not, look at the object again, noticing more of the details, and close your eyes again. With your eyes closed, try to "zoom-in" on the image and notice the lines, colors, dimensions, etc.

If this seems a little mind-boggling, here is a slight variation: close your eyes and think about what your TV or computer monitor looks like. Sometimes when you turn a TV off, the picture shrinks down to a little white dot in the middle of the screen. Put a "white dot" in the center of your mental TV. Imagine that dot gradually getting larger until it fills the screen, and as it grows, imagine seeing the object you were trying to visualize earlier.

If you still don't "see" the mental image, try leaving your eyes open and defocusing. If you have ever looked out across the distance or at a blank wall and noticed that your mind wandered somewhere else where you weren't seeing the distant scenery or the wall, this "daydreaming" state is what I mean by defocusing. Try "daydreaming" the object.

Another variation is to use the telephoto lens technique. When you look at the object, notice that you can zoom-in on a particular aspect of the object, or zoom-out to see the scene in its entirety. When you close your eyes, try zooming in on various aspects of your mental image to see them more clearly and then zoom back out again. Alternating between looking at the object and closing your eyes may help you refine your visualization incrementally.

It may also help to start with very simple objects like the letter 'A.' Write this letter on a piece of paper and then try to see it in your mind's eye.

Another way to chunk this learning process down is to focus on a single color at a time. For example, look at a tree, then close your eyes and try to mentally match the exact shade of green.

If this seems difficult, mark your calendar to try this exercise again tomorrow, in a week, or even a month. You may be surprised that taking mental snapshots is easier after your subconscious mind has had time to "incubate" the technique.

What I like best about this exercise is that it can be done during what would otherwise be wasted time ("rice time"). For example, I sometimes do it while waiting in a reception area with nothing to read, or while standing in a line where it is safe to close my eyes for a few seconds.

VISUALIZATION EXERCISE #2: SUBMODALITIES

➜   Imagine that you are watching TV and all of the sudden the picture starts getting smaller and smaller until it's the size of a postage stamp. How motivated would you be to watch your program with the image that small? Then all of the sudden the picture starts getting larger, returns back to normal, but continues to "zoom-in" so that only a small portion of the normal image fills the screen. It's okay with you though, because it zoomed in on the face of your favorite character.

In the blink of an eye the picture zooms back to normal and then begins to blur. This makes it harder and harder to tell what is going on and again decreases your motivation to watch the program. Just when it's almost unbearable, the situation reverses itself and the focus returns. Not only that, but as it focuses, the colors and light seem to be getting brighter and brighter, adding a more cheerful atmosphere to the show.

Then a sad scene begins, but to your surprise, the scene suddenly converts to a cartoon and assumes a more playful tone. The sad scene ends in a way you don't like, so you play the cartoon backwards until it gets to the beginning. When it starts going forward again, you make things turn out much better. Finally, you decide to do something else, so you grab the mental image of the TV and throw it behind you in order to get it off your mind.

What I just described doing with a mental image of a TV program you can do with any mental image you can remember or create. This is another groundbreaking Neuro Linguistic Programming (NLP) technique taught by Richard Bandler and John Grinder in their book, *Frogs into Princes*, and in Richard Bandler's *Using Your Brain* book and audiotape. "Modalities" (visual, auditory, kinesthetic, olfactory, and gustatory) are the major categories by which we represent the external world in our mind. We form mental maps of the external world using mental pictures, sounds, feelings, smells and tastes. In this way we "re-present" external reality to our mind, and take actions based upon this internal map or re-presentation. Everybody's internal map is different, primarily because the external world is so infinitely complex. We form mental models that approximate what our senses perceive, and these models drive our behavior.

Modalities are the major modes of mentally mapping external reality. Submodalities are the attributes used within each major mode of thinking. If you did the TV exercise above, then you adjusted the following visual submodalities: size of image, focus, brightness, location, speed at which the scenes were played, and whether or not it was a cartoon or real-life. These are just a few of the submodalities you can vary. Others include viewpoint (the angle from which you are observing the picture), proximity (how close you are to the image), whether the image has a frame around it or goes on forever like the wrap-around screen at Disney World, and whether or not you are in the picture or watching from a distance.

This exercise involved only visual submodalities. You can also change the attributes of the sounds you "hear" in your head and the feelings you sense internally. *Awaken the Giant Within* by Anthony Robbins contains an excellent one-page checklist of visual, auditory and kinesthetic submodalities. Richard Bandler's book and audiotape, *Using Your Brain,* are also excellent sources for further study. The audiotape version of *Using Your Brain* gives extensive examples of how to expand your use of auditory submodalities. Bandler tells of a time when he fell asleep with the TV on. At four in the morning, a station came on playing a loud classical music concert. While most people would think that the TV came on and woke them up, Bandler just thought that he had woken up, because that is what his internal experience is like— frequently playing motivational, multi-instrument concerts in his head.

I believe that the techniques provided by Neuro Linguistic Programming (NLP) are so profound, that even after 20 years of research and application, we are still just beginning to realize their full potential. So many books have encouraged us to visualize what we want. Bandler and Grinder analyzed the structure of subjective experience and said, "here's how". The potential applications of NLP are so vast and unexplored that this is an excellent area to use "mastermind" energy discussed in the next chapter to accelerate your understanding and application of this material.

In addition to being an excellent technique for developing your visual muscle, there are many ways you can apply submodality skills to knowledge work. For example, when visualizing you can experiment to discover which submodalities have the greatest impact on your motivation and/or energy level. Think of your office at work. Do you have a dark, dingy picture of this place, or is it bright, large, highly focused, and very close to your face? When you think of your workplace, what emotional response does it invoke? Does that emotional response contribute to or detract from your ability to deliver value to your customers? You may want to experiment with various submodalities in order to optimize this emotional response. What would happen if every time you walked in your office door, the song "Chariots of Fire" (or some other song that motivates you) began blasting at 70 decibels in your mind?

Stephen Covey encourages us to "Begin with the end in mind." Neuro Linguistic Programming teaches us to ask: "*How* can I represent this end in my mind in such a way that it inspires me to give my best performance on a moment by moment basis?"

"How many of you ever thought about the possibility of intentionally varying the brightness of an internal image in order to feel different? Most of you just let your brain randomly show you any picture it wants, and you feel good or bad in response."

— Richard Bandler

You may recall those attachments that fit on the end of a garden hose, so that when the water is turned on, it starts whipping around wildly, spraying water every which way while the children run around trying to "avoid" getting sprayed. Well, in some cases this is how people run their minds, waiting for external circumstances to occur that trigger certain thoughts, or just letting whatever thought that comes along occupy their consciousness. It's unpredictable and can sometimes be fun, but as a predominant way of thinking, this mental strategy can lead to disappointment. To take control of your submodalities is to grab that hose and focus the water like a laser beam in the direction you want to go!

VISUALIZATION EXERCISE #3: DRAWING

→   As Betty Edwards teaches in her book, *Drawing on the Right Side of the Brain,* learning to draw involves learning to see things in a different way. I believe learning to draw can also help you improve visualization skills.

This exercise involves picking an object or a scene and looking at it until you see it clearly enough to draw it. The quality of the drawing becomes a feedback mechanism for the clarity of your vision. Here are some guidelines:

1) Initially, set a time limit such as 10 minutes, and then stick to that. My experience has been that it is easy to lose track of time when I'm in "right-brain" mode. As explained in Chapter 5, each side of our brain specializes in certain activities. The left is usually more linear, and thus more adept with linear time. Most people use the right brain for non-linear thinking such as drawing or perceiving dimension.

2) Use a thick leaded pencil. Drawing with a .5 mm mechanical pencil is more difficult.

3) Keep a large eraser handy and use it as much as needed to refine your drawing.

4) Alternate between focusing on the image and then defocusing. Each time, try to "notice" more and more details of the image.

5) Before starting to draw, make a few coordinate dots to mark the outer boundaries. For example, if you are drawing a tree, place a dot at the tree's highest point and a few dots to mark the perimeter and where the trunk begins. These coordinates provide a framework for guiding your drawing.

6) If light is reflecting off a certain portion of the object, draw it as if it wasn't and use an eraser to lighten the reflecting area.

7) Close your eyes and move your mental image of the object around in your internal visual sphere. Notice if it

is easier to clarify the image in any of the positions. For example, if your visual screen is like a large white board, try moving the image to the upper left corner, upper right, straight ahead, to your left, etc. If your visual screen is like a wraparound movie screen, try moving it to your direct left, right, or putting it above you. Finally, if your visual screen is like virtual reality, try walking through the image and looking at it from several different angles.

8) Give the exercise and drawing positive energy. This is the opposite of dreading the experience. Think about how grateful you are for the opportunity to explore a new skill with so many processional benefits in other areas of thinking. Think about the scene you are drawing with as much admiration and awe as you can generate. Appreciate what had to happen for that scene to exist before you. Instead of resisting the process, let this positive energy flow into a brighter, fuller, more detailed internal image of the scene. Then let this positive energy flow through your hand into your drawing. You can learn more about using positive energy in James Redfield's book, *The Celestine Prophecy*.

9) Get a copy of Betty Edward's, *Drawing on the Right Side of the Brain*, an excellent book on the subject which has sold more than 1.2 million copies.

As Richard Bandler points out, a major benefit of the visual system is that you can easily see two different pictures simultaneously. It's much harder to pay attention to two voices at once.

Visualization Exercise #4:
Ten-Minute Visualization

➔ While working on developing a software application, I frequently use ten-minute visualization sessions which go something like this:

1) I look at my watch and create a mental image of what the clock will look like at the end of the ten minute period. My watch is both digital and analog, so I prefer to use the stop watch feature to help ensure that I'm out of there exactly when my designated time limit is up.

2) I find an empty office or conference room where I won't be disturbed (how about designating a small office as a visualization room?). I find I need a comfortable temperature and the less noise the better. My ears have become so sensitized to the sound of computer fans that I either have to go to a quiet office or shut off my computer before I can use my office. In the summer months, I sometimes use the reclined passenger seat in my car.

3) I turn out the lights or I put something over my eyes to block the light.

4) I lay on the floor (only if it's clean and not heavily traveled—you may want to use a towel) or on the conference table.

5) I sometimes do a little light stretching of my lower back to help trigger a relaxation response.

6) I begin with a couple complete breaths as taught by yoga instructor Richard Hittleman. Begin a complete breath by exhaling completely. Without hesitation, begin filling your lower lungs with air. When your abdominal region won't expand any further, fill your chest with air. Hold for a few seconds, exhale completely, then repeat without pausing at the point of

full exhalation. Complete breathing generates Prana or "life force".

7) I then visualize the software working the way I want it to. I imagine somebody actually using the software, clicking the mouse and selecting menu options and clicking buttons. Screens get repainted, new forms pop up, etc. If you work in a field other than software, then step into the future to the day after your project has been successfully completed. Imagine how life would be different for your customers as they use the results of your work. In as much detail as possible, see them using and benefiting from your work. If it seems difficult, first realize that it may be because you are working on a difficult project—but realize that this is the process of creating something new. All things are created twice: first in someone's mind and then in reality. Sometimes it takes several visualization sessions over time to evolve a clear mental picture.

8) Also note that while visualizing in these ten-minute sessions, I sometimes oscillate between focused visualization and "going with the flow". In other words, I may invest a few minutes consciously working through the screens, and then let go of the mental steering wheel. I clear my mind with some focused breathing, and just notice what related ideas drift into my consciousness. After a couple of minutes of this, I'll switch back into focused visualization in order to integrate the new ideas my subconscious mind has come up with during the pause.

While this may sound a bit weird, when I work on a project, what matters is successfully completing the project. This technique helps me do this—especially on the more difficult projects. It also gives my back a rest.

For more advanced exercises on developing your visualization muscle, refer to Chapter 17 in *Superlearning*, by Sheila Ostrander and Lynn Schroeder. It's no accident that this book has sold over a million copies! Kevin Trudeau's

Mega Memory tapes also contain good exercises for developing this skill.

"Some things you see with your eyes, others you must see with your heart."

— from the movie, Land Before Time

DEVELOP METAPHOR SKILLS

➔   The second major strategy for effective self-communication involves metaphors. Metaphors are used extensively in this book to convey meaning—the essence of what I'm trying to say—very quickly. My aim is to use things you are already familiar with as a bridge to new ideas I'm presenting (river of increasing swiftness, brain dancing, etc.). This section describes how you can apply this same technique to communicate direction to your subconscious mind at higher bandwidths.

Many consider Milton Erickson to have been the greatest hypnotherapist who ever lived. Hypnotherapists are masters at communicating directly with the subconscious mind. Bandler and Grinder originated many of their breakthrough ideas from studying the work of Erickson and Virginia Satir. In his book about Erickson called *Taproots*, William O'Hanlon writes that the word metaphor is derived from the Greek roots *pherin* meaning 'to carry' and *meta*, which means 'beyond' or 'over.' "The function of metaphor is to carry knowledge across contexts, beyond its initial context into a new one."

According to O'Hanlon, Erickson believed that people already have the abilities needed to solve their problems. Erickson's task in therapy was to transfer this know-how across contexts, from the one(s) in which the patient currently has it to the context which he does not. He accomplished this by using metaphor in its various forms. Similarly, we can use metaphors to enhance the effectiveness of our "self-communication".

Thinking in metaphors is a skill, and I owe a lot to R.L. Wing, author of *The TAO of Power*, for accelerating my learning journey in this area. In this translation of Lao Tzu's classic, *Tao Te Ching*, Wing suggests that you identify an event, transaction, relationship or revelation that stands out on your path through life. Then "pull back your mind from the details of the situation" and describe it using a metaphor from nature. "For example," he writes, "a dead-end position that forced you to change careers might find an analogy in a river pouring into a box canyon and eventually overflowing to form a new waterway."

From this perspective, life is full of lessons. For example, in 1992, I was standing barefoot on the shore of the Pacific Ocean. I knew that I wanted to make a major shift in my career direction by writing this book and doing related activities, yet it was proving difficult to imagine how I could pull off the transition. While standing ankle deep in the water, I noticed that about every third wave was larger and went much farther up the sand. What was happening was that a couple smaller waves would come in and form a base as they retreated. Then a third wave would come along and ride on top of what was left of the first two, in order to extend its reach up the beach. I realized that I could use a multiphase approach to the transition, whereby each phase would provide a base for the "third wave" that would take me where I wanted to go.

Next time you get stuck on a project, think of a metaphor in nature that enriches your perspective. Having a broad knowledge base about nature gives you more reference material for metaphors.

Personal experiences also serve as great source of metaphors. My uncle once described a situation where he and two other men needed to move a large boulder that had rolled onto the road. Their initial efforts didn't budge it and the other two men began to walk away. On a hunch, he suggested that the two men return and try again. He was able to convince them that they could move the boulder and this time they were successful.

Two years later, when he needed to move some railroad ties, after initial difficulty, he remembered the time he and his friends moved the boulder from the road. By vividly remembering the details of that experience, he was able to tap into similar resources and lift the heavy objects. His previous experience served as a metaphor that he used to communicate to his subconscious in a way that allowed him to lift the objects. The interesting thing about these incidents is that this lifting was accomplished without a huge rush of adrenaline. There is still much to learn about the type of energy my uncle employed in these situations.

While working on complex projects, there have been several instances where a task seemed beyond my reach. When this happens, I remember previous projects where I experienced similar feelings and yet somehow managed to complete the work. Such reference experiences increase my belief that I will succeed this time as well. It also helps to remember the overall process I used to get over the hurdle. In this way, personal experiences are also a great source of metaphors for high bandwidth self-communication.

DEVELOP FULL PHYSIOLOGY AFFIRMATION SKILLS

→   The third major strategy for effective self-communication involves affirmations. Earlier in this chapter I wrote that there were two dimensions to self-communication: what you are thinking and how you are using your physiology. This section summarizes the basic rules of affirmations and emphasizes a related distinction pioneered by Anthony Robbins that is not as well known.

In his book *The Power of Your Subconscious Mind*, Dr. Joseph Murphy states that "motion and emotion must balance." What Anthony Robbins did was apply this to the nth degree. While this is just one of Anthony Robbins' optimum performance strategies, I believe it has played a significant role in his considerable success.

So what does he do differently? Robbins uses affirmations during moments that he has generated powerful physiologies. For example, he describes how he used to run along the beach in California saying his affirmations over and over again. As he ran, he said his affirmations with all of the intensity he could muster. Robbins also uses this distinction to achieve a peak state before going on stage to speak. The following is an adaptation of one of Robbins' affirmations that has worked well for me:

> I now command my subconscious mind to direct me in helping as many people as possible today, by giving me the STRENGTH!, POWER!!, BREVITY!!!, HUMOR!!!!, EMOTION!!!!!, whatever it takes, to motivate these people to take action that will improve their lives NOW!!!!!!!!!!!!!!!!!!!!!"

The "!" in the above affirmation stands for "say with all the emotional intensity and power you can generate." This emotional charge can be significantly amplified with powerful physiology. Some of the components of this physiology are strong breathing, strong congruent posture, physical gestures that encourage a sense of resourcefulness, and the use of your 80 facial muscles. Your whole physiology should encourage feelings of highly focused determination.

"Emotion is created by motion."

— Anthony Robbins

"In fact," writes Napoleon Hill, "there is much evidence to support that only emotionalized thoughts have any action influence on the subconscious mind." Why? Because most people are constantly talking to themselves. Your subconscious must have some way of distinguishing between the mental chit-chat and the really important stuff. Emotionally charging your affirmations is one such way of signaling to your subconscious to pay attention. And because emotion is created by motion, powerful congruent physiologies are one "lever" you can use to get your subconscious mind's attention.

The only way you can truly appreciate the effectiveness with which Robbins "peaks" himself is to actually watch him in action. Robbins is by far the most effective public speaker I've ever observed. According to his infomercial, one company paid him $100,000 for a one day seminar! I highly recommend that you attend one of his seminars both for its content, which is consistently first rate, and to observe his public speaking abilities, which set a new standard for us all.

In her book, *Creative Visualization*, Shakti Gawain states: "In general, the shorter and simpler the affirmation, the more effective." It should be a clear statement that conveys a strong feeling—the more feeling it conveys, the stronger impression it will make on your mind. Long, wordy and theoretical affirmations lose their emotional impact. She encourages you to choose affirmations that come from your heart, not your head.

"A good affirmation has five basic ingredients:" says Stephen Covey, "it's personal, it's positive, it's present tense, it's visual, and it's emotional." Applying this formula I came up with two affirmations: "It is deeply satisfying that my book helps people work smarter and live more balanced lives," and, "It is deeply satisfying that I write highly useful, concise, fun-to-read ideas that help others work smarter." While saying these affirmations, I visualize people thanking me for making a positive contribution to their lives.

Shakti Gawain also suggests that you only use affirmations that feel right to you. "When using affirmations, try as much as possible to create a feeling of belief, an experience that they can be true." The implied message I get from Anthony Robbins is that he is able to create and associate to feelings of strong belief more easily when he is in his most powerful and resourceful physiologies.

Two affirmations I used frequently while writing *Brain Dancing* are: "*Brain Dancing* inspires effective mental action now!" and "*Brain Dancing* mobilizes untapped intellectual resources of knowledge workers!" While running along the shores of Lake Washington, I repeated these two affirmations with all the intensity I could muster. Sometimes I would say these affirmations just in my mind. However, saying them out loud in a strong voice involves more physiology and is more effective, even though you may get a strange look or two.

I have conditioned myself such that each time I turn a certain corner to where I can first see the rippling water of the lake, the affirmations begin in my mind automatically. In Neuro Linguistic Programming, this is referred to as "anchoring". You may know a song or two that remind you of certain people, places or events. Those songs are auditory anchors. At the time you first heard them (or heard them several times), you were probably experiencing some strong emotions. The important thing to notice is that you are reminded of these experiences without even having to try. Thinking about them is automatic.

I like to think of this process of building resourceful anchors as if I'm climbing a mountain. Each time I use this powerful running physiology to generate strong emotions and then anchor it in, it is like pounding a spike into the rock face. When I engage that anchor next time, it propels me back to that spot on the mountain. From there I can climb a little higher by intensifying the emotional state while seeing the visual stimulus (Lake Washington), thus pounding another spike a little higher up the mountainside.

Anchoring offers you the opportunity to leverage your will power by creating "push button" emotions. The above example is just one of the many types of anchors you can create. Here are the basic rules for creating effective anchors:

- You need a unique stimulus, which can be visual, auditory, kinesthetic, olfactory or gustatory.
- You must be in a peak state when you see the sight, hear the sound, feel the touch, taste the taste, or smell the smell.

- You must be able to reproduce the stimulus precisely in order to engage the anchor.

To apply this distinction, pick a spot on your running path where you turn a corner and see something unique. (If you are not a runner, you could try walking strongly and directly.) It should be a point along your run where you are in peak physiology—running strongly. As soon as you turn the corner, begin saying your affirmation with all the intensity you can muster, while focusing on this unique visual stimulus. Say the affirmations out loud if it helps. Sometimes I shout them in my mind. If you invest the conscious energy the first time or two, you won't have to consciously remember to make your affirmations while you run in the future. They will begin in your mind automatically when you see that particular scene. To access this resourceful physiology in other situations, you can mentally relive the experience of turning the corner, seeing that unique visual stimulus in your mind's eye, and saying your affirmation in the same way you do while running.

Anchors have many applications beyond this example. For example, on the Bill Moyer's PBS television show *Healing and the Mind*, a young girl had a serious illness for which the only medication was a drug known to have serious side effects. In order to get her off this medication as soon as possible, she smelled camphor each time she took the medicine. The message to her body was: "when you smell this, do this." Eventually, the girl got to the point where all she had to do was smell the camphor, and her body was able to reproduce the healing effect (or healing state) encouraged by the medicine. The smell triggered her body's memory of the healing response.

To recap then, repeat affirmations while in peak physiology and use anchors to make each affirmation an investment in your future resources.

Type	Cycles/ Second	Typical Mental Activity
Delta	.5 - 3	Large and slow. Deep, dreamless sleep.
Theta	4 - 7	Seem to be involved in emotionality, creative imagery, and computation on a deep level. Rarely occur while awake.
Alpha	8 - 13	Associated with an alert but relaxed state of mind. Most people produce alpha waves when they close their eyes, but the typical waking, eyes-open EEG shows alpha waves mixed with other patterns. Steady alpha waves are uncommon in one whose eyes are open.
Beta	14 - 30	Fast, tight pattern occurs during logical thought, analysis, action, and normal conversation.

Figure 3.1. Brain wave frequencies.

DEVELOP THE ABILITY TO GET INTO ALPHA STATE

➜ The last major strategy for effective self-communication involves generating alpha brain waves. This is the complementary opposite of full physiology affirmations. As explained in Chapter 1, one of the many spectrums of thought involve brain wave frequencies. The brain produces electrochemical impulses which travel 3 to 400 feet per second. For comparison, electric current in your house travels nearly the speed of light (186,282 mi/sec). First discovered in 1929 by Hans Berger, these brain waves have since been categorized as shown in Figure 3.1.

I would add a fifth category, "Nuclear Beta". It does not show up in any other literature. I have no idea how many cycles are in one second, but it seems accelerated to me. I made this up to describe what seems to happen to my mental activity when I deliver a speech energetically or am involved in another form of synergistic dialogue.

Self-communication is a two-way street. My research suggests that alpha brain waves can enhance both the process of communicating a desired outcome to your subconscious mind, as well as listening in on the guidance your subconscious sends back as a result of this directional information. In either case, the process of generating alpha brain waves is the same. The difference is what you do once you have reached this state.

Generating alpha brain waves is a skill that can be developed by progressing through the four stages involved in learning any new skill:

1) Unconscious Incompetence.
2) Conscious Incompetence.
3) Conscious Competence.
4) Unconscious Competence.

Unconscious incompetence is where you don't know what you don't know. Conscious incompetence is where you become aware that you don't know how to do something that you have a desire to learn. Conscious competence is where you can do the task, but only by devoting all of your attention to it. The fourth stage, unconscious competence, is the stage where you can do the task without having to think about it much, if at all. Just as you learned to drive a car, you can learn to drive your subconscious mind with alpha brain waves.

"Much of therapy is tipping the first domino."

— Milton Erickson

Over one million people have graduated from the Silva Mind Control Training developed by José Silva. I haven't taken this course, but I've experienced good results from applying the techniques suggested in his excellent book, *The Silva Mind*

Control Method. Silva suggests using alpha state to do "dynamic meditation" employing the trilogy of desire, belief and expectancy.

However, in her landmark book, *The Brain Revolution,* Marilyn Ferguson wrote, "Mentally visualizing an object in minute detail usually blocks alpha production, for example, just as actual visual observation does." Given this contradictory information, I suggest experimenting with both approaches to see what works for you. Shakti Gawain, whose work in this area I respect, endorses the Silva Method classes. Perhaps visualizing while staying in alpha is a skill we can develop. The new biofeedback devices such as the "Mind Mirror," which measure the output of each hemisphere for each category of brain wave, may help us refine such skills.

If you have never meditated or done "relaxed visualization," it may be a bit out of your comfort zone. You may want to try a three-phase approach:

- Use 10-minute power naps to develop the ability to relax mid-day.
- Do relaxed visualization immediately upon awakening in the morning.
- Use meditation to "tune-in" to subconscious guidance.

Ten minute power naps are described in Chapter 5. I am fairly certain that I go into alpha state during these naps, from which I often awaken feeling as if I'd just gotten the best full night's sleep of my life. I know that sounds like an exaggeration, but I've talked to several other people who have had a similar experience. This is not a visualization exercise, but it does help you develop the ability to shift gears in the middle of the day into a relaxed state. Relaxation is an important aspect of getting into an alpha state.

The "morning visualization" approach leverages on the fact that alpha state, or the state of mind and body which produces alpha brain waves, is common just after waking. With this exercise, it is important that you establish a means of limiting the duration. You don't want to fall back asleep and risk being late for work, since we tend to avoid exercises which are not ecological for us. One solution is to use a snooze button cycle on your alarm clock. For more control over duration, you could use a second alarm clock set ten minutes later, or one of the his/her clocks that let you set two alarms.

This strategy is the complete opposite of the "full physiology affirmation" approach discussed in the previous section. Whereas that approach involved whipping yourself into an emotional frenzy, this strategy involves visualizing your desired outcome in a state of relaxed alertness. By quieting the mind, you reduce interference, and the messages you send your subconscious are better understood. There is less background noise for your subconscious to filter out. I don't know exactly why this method improves visualization effectiveness. Here are some suggestions adapted from José Silva's book, *The Silva Mind Control Method* that you may want to try:

1) Set your alarm for 15 minutes.
2) Continue to breathe in a very relaxed way.
3) Close your eyes and look upward at a 20 degree angle.
4) Slowly count backward from 100 to 1, at 2 second intervals. As you get better at it, you can decrease to 50 and eventually to just 3. Keep your mind only on the counting. Here's where discipline comes in.
5) When you get to 1, you will have reached some level of an alpha state. It is at this point that Silva suggests going beyond traditional meditation, which he acknowledges is significant in and of itself. He suggests that this state is also an excellent opportunity to develop your visualization skills. You can do this by placing a simple image on your "mental screen," such as an apple, or work on visualizing a desired outcome in vivid detail.
6) Your results will be significantly influenced by the degree to which you desire the outcome, believe that the

event can take place, and expect that it will occur. In addition, Silva states that this technique cannot be used to "assist in an evil design," such as one that causes harm to others.

7) Use the following routine to come out of your meditative state. Say to yourself: "I will slowly come out as I count from one to five, feeling wide awake and better than before." Open your eyes on the count of three, and become wide awake on the count of five.

Silva encourages you to be consistent from day one as to how you go in and come out of alpha. This will help you develop anchors, or condition yourself to go in and out of the desired state more rapidly. Eventually, you can develop the ability to go into this alpha state anytime during the day. If this counting down technique does not work for you, try visualizing a clear blue sky. Marilyn Ferguson's research suggests that the alpha rhythm is encouraged when the brain is scanning for a pattern. However, she also points out that some individuals can perform tasks such as speed reading and mathematical computation without reducing alpha production. Perhaps your own experiments will help shed some light on this potentially high leverage mental activity.

Self-communication is a two-way street, yet everything in this chapter so far has dealt with communicating *to* your subconscious mind. One of the many uses of more traditional meditation is receiving guidance *from* your subconscious. The final section in this chapter addresses the issue of intuition.

INTUITION:
LISTENING TO SUBCONSCIOUS GUIDANCE

I think of intuition as the process by which our subconscious mind sends us messages, some of which are in response to the directional information we have self-communicated to our subconscious. The best book I've found on intuition is called *The Intuitive Edge* by Philip Goldberg. Shakti Gawain's writings touch on many related themes as well, such as her book *Creative Visualization.*

> *"Intuition is to be tempted, not pursued."*
>
> — *Philip Goldberg*

As Marilyn Ferguson writes in *The Aquarian Conspiracy,* "If we are to use our capacities fully and confidently...we must recognize the power of intuition. Our very technology has generated so many options that only intuition can help us choose." The basic premise I operate on is that the subconscious mind is the seat of action. When we take action, our subconscious mind is making zillions of decisions on the fly. In multimedia technology, there is a concept known as "streaming", whereby video images are transferred directly from the CD-ROM to the video driver, bypassing the computer's CPU (Central Processing Unit). To do otherwise would slow the computer down considerably. The process of managing the interplay between the conscious and subconscious looks something like the following. You use the various techniques presented in this chapter to create a "multimedia" title in your subconscious mind. As you go about the day, your subconscious plays back this title in the form of actions that bypass conscious processing, at least to some degree, and your actions are guided to take you in the direction defined in your subconscious multimedia title.

During this process, interpreting the signals our subconscious sends us can be challenging. For example, life is full of temptations pulling us every which way. Determining which signals are intuitive guidance and which are influenced by environmental circumstances can be difficult. Traditional forms of meditation can help a person be more "tuned-in" to their intuition. Goldberg recommends Transcendental Meditation, as does Deepak Chopra, author of *Quantum Healing* and promoter of Ayurvedic health principles. Transcendental Meditation classes cost several hundred dollars, so I've chosen to develop my meditation skills through books, audiotapes, and by interviewing people who meditate regularly.

Goldberg suggests that we reward bold ideas slightly off mark in order to create an adventurous attitude conducive to intuitive insights. He notes that without exception, the people he interviewed have their most significant intuitive experiences while away from work. For Mozart, this occurred while traveling, going for walks, or during the night when he couldn't sleep. "*Whence* and *how* they come, I know not; nor can I force them," wrote Mozart. Goldberg concludes, "...a well-timed incubation period seems to be good bait for intuition."

This idea forms one of the major underlying themes of Chapter 5, Synergistic Oscillation. I get a surprising number of ideas while stretching after a workout or doing some other disciplined act, such as turning down a sweet that is particularly tempting. Stretching is the part of my workout that requires the most discipline. However, when I'm cruising in the San Juan Islands, I am so far removed from my work that I can't recall this time being a major source of business related ideas. My work, often highly technical and detail-oriented, requires a great deal of concentration. While boating, I defocus my mind, relax my concentration muscle, and go with the flow of the experience—very much the opposite of my mindset at work. I do get high-level ideas while on these trips, and when I return to work, these periods of mental rest recharge my mental batteries. This allows me to deal with technical issues with more proficiency and mental clarity. Mental rest is discussed further in Chapter 5.

By far my greatest source of useful ideas while working on projects has been the discussions I have with my teammates. I am not saying that the ideas come from my teammates. I am saying that they come from the process of discussing issues with them. There have been many times when I've gotten several ideas from discussions where the other person never even says a word!

Intuition is a broad subject and tough to pin down. Readers interested in pursuing this topic further should consult the books mentioned above. I sum up my strategy for using intuition in knowledge work as follows:

- Clearly communicate your desired project outcome to your subconscious using the strategies discussed in this chapter. This is "sowing the seeds".

- Use "synergistic oscillation" strategies discussed in Chapter 5 to further nurture your intuitive resources. Developing the mental flexibility and discipline to quiet the mind in a meditative state is one of the fundamental skills for "tempting" intuition and for developing your ability to "tune-in" to intuitive guidance.

- Use "synergistic dialogue" as discussed in the next chapter to reap the rewards of your self-communication efforts.

CHAPTER 4

SYNERGISTIC DIALOGUE

"Human beings have an extraordinary capacity to think together."

— *Peter Senge*

➜   Executives surveyed in 1995 by USA Today reported that
they get most of their new ideas while talking with people.
Something special happens to our thinking when two or more
people discuss an issue they care about. Something special
that increases our access to a pool of intelligence not readily
available while thinking alone. Many people seem to
underestimate the true potential of this distinction. I don't
remember seeing "idea flow management" listed as an
objective of any interpersonal communication skills course.
My goal with this chapter is to help you get to the point
where you can brainstorm on the fly in virtually any
conversation, the second major strategy for using
complementary opposites to achieve mental leverage.

Conscious ⟵⟶ Subconscious
Individual Thought ⟵⟶ **Dialogue**
Left-Brain Mode ⟵⟶ Right-Brain Mode
Detailed Thought ⟵⟶ High Level Thought

After giving you an overview of the best teachings I've found
on this subject, the five main ways I use synergistic dialogue
are summarized. The majority of this chapter covers
suggestions for applying this idea within project teams.

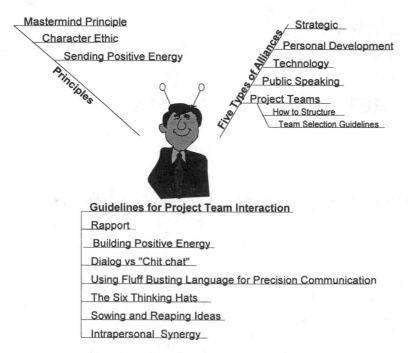

Figure 4.1. Mindmap of Chapter 4.

PRINCIPLES

NAPOLEON HILL'S MASTERMIND PRINCIPLE

➔ In *Think and Grow Rich,* one of the all-time best-selling business books, Napoleon Hill states, "No two minds ever come together without, thereby, creating a third, invisible, intangible force which may be likened to a third mind." Hill discovered that the mastermind principle was a key strategy of several highly successful business leaders such as Andrew Carnegie, Henry Ford, and Thomas Edison. His basic message was to form alliances with individuals who have knowledge and mental capacities complimentary to your own. The more brain power and the more they care about the issue, the better. Once you've located such individuals, arrange to meet with them on a regular basis for purposes of developing and refining strategic plans.

Hill believed that each person's brain is both a broadcasting and receiving station. Thought vibrations released by one brain may be picked up and interpreted by all other brains that are in 'tune' with the broadcasting brain. While discussing issues with your mastermind group, the rate of thinking of group members is "stepped up" in a way that increases the degree to which they can tune-in to thoughts released by other brains.

When I first read this, I began searching for people interested in forming such alliances. What took me a little longer to realize was that every conversation can benefit from this distinction to some degree. That last sentence is worth reading again, because it has played a critical role in every project I've worked on. Being able to form mini-mastermind groups on the fly is the most important interpersonal communications skill a knowledge worker can develop.

You know you are applying the mastermind principle correctly when your "rate of thinking" is stepped up such that ideas begin to flow into your mind during conversation. When you verbalize these ideas to the group, it fuels further conversation that evolves into useful knowledge. I refer to this stepped up rate of thinking as "nuclear beta," because it feels very different from both alpha and normal beta consciousness. What is needed to confirm this pattern is a way to monitor brain waves while a person is giving a speech. At least for me, this is when the phenomena seems most pronounced.

Oftentimes we can increase our awareness of certain ideas by experiencing their opposite. The opposite of the mastermind effect can be experienced by delivering a speech to a blank wall. One reason this requires so much discipline is that the energizing and amplifying effect of the audience is missing.

As an exercise, the next time you have the opportunity to speak to a group, pause for a moment before you begin to speak and notice if ideas seem to present themselves to you. These ideas may not seem related to what you are going to say, but they usually turn out to be brilliantly related. You must exercise faith when you do this. You must believe that ideas will come to you as necessary for effective communication. This experience, even if you only speak for one minute, is a microcosm representing the essence of one of the most profound lessons a person can learn.

One way to experiment with "nuclear beta" is to attend a Toastmasters meeting and volunteer to participate in "Table Topics". This is the part of the meetings where members practice impromptu speaking. The designated "Table Topics Master" arrives at each meeting with a list of prepared subjects or questions. After the main speeches for the meeting have been delivered, there is a break while the evaluators prepare their responses. During this time, the Table Topics Master calls on individuals at random who must stand up and give a 30-second to 1½-minute talk on this subject off the top of their head. Now this is truly faith in action. The more you are willing to trust that ideas will come to you, the more they seem to flow in abundance. Rather than sitting and fretting about what you might say in such situations, you can look forward to the "idea burst" that occurs and for the opportunity to develop your "faith muscle". Non-members are given the option to decline the invitation to speak in case you would just like to observe the process the first time you attend. At the time of this writing, there are over 8,000 clubs worldwide. To locate the Toastmasters group nearest you, or for information on how to start your own club, call (800) 993-7732.

Peter Senge, Director of the Systems Thinking and Organizational Learning Program at MIT's Sloan School of Management, sums it up beautifully with the words: "Human beings have an extraordinary capacity to think together." In his landmark book, *The Fifth Discipline*, Senge describes this phenomena as dialogue—a type of conversation whereby the group "becomes open to the flow of a larger intelligence".

Senge quotes the physicist, Werner Heisenberg (formulator of the famous "Uncertainty Principle" in modern physics) as saying that "Science is rooted in conversations. The cooperation of different people may culminate in scientific results of the utmost importance." In his book *Physics and Beyond: Encounters and Conversations*, Heisenberg recalls how conversations with Pauli, Einstein, Bohr, and others had a lasting effect on his thinking, and literally gave birth to many of the theories for which these men eventually became famous. Senge's *Fifth Discipline* audiotape series also contains excellent ideas on the subject of dialogue.

"There is this idea factory to which I subscribe."

— Isaac Asimov

We don't know for sure where ideas come from when engaged in dialogue. Are we immersed in a sea of infinite intelligence, to which the extra energy provided in synergistic dialogue helps us tune in? Or is it that our minds simply have access to more internal resources when provided with this energy? For knowledge workers, knowing where the ideas come from is not as important as knowing how to lure them into consciousness. It is to this end that I direct the majority of this chapter. How does a person prepare themselves for the mental leverage that can come from applying the mastermind principle? What can a person do to encourage the flow of ideas to others in conversation? To answer these questions we must turn to Stephen Covey and James Redfield.

CHARACTER ETHIC: PREPARING YOURSELF FOR SYNERGY

➔ You can enhance your ability to receive ideas in conversation, and help others do the same, by nurturing the habits Stephen Covey describes in his book, *The 7 Habits of Highly Effective People*. Habit #6, synergistic communication, occurs among two or more individuals when there is a high degree of trust and cooperation. Covey says that you don't aim for synergy, but rather you focus on habits number 4 (seek first to understand then to be understood) and 5 (think win/win) and synergy results.

After centering your personal security on the degree to which you have aligned your habits with the fundamental principles governing our lives, you are more likely to be able to participate in dialogue without being threatened by the ideas of others. Being able to generate ideas in the presence of others is nurtured by abolishing the fear of appearing stupid. I am constantly tossing out "off the wall" ideas; some of them are useful, many are lousy. Oftentimes it is a variation of such lousy ideas that ends up solving the problem. Covey's habits present a road map for building a sense of worth based on your alignment with principles as opposed to what others might think.

"SENDING POSITIVE ENERGY" IN DIALOGUE

➔   Napoleon Hill made us aware that the "mastermind principle" exists, Stephen Covey gave us a strategy to prepare ourselves for synergistic dialogue by developing our character, and recently, James Redfield has taken us another step on this journey by explaining the energy dynamics of conversation itself. In his book, *The Celestine Prophecy*, Redfield describes the process by which you can support or send energy to other meeting participants. He describes how this energy can flow from person to person as a conversation evolves. If you have ever spoken to a group and felt like someone in the audience was throwing mental darts at you, then you have experienced the opposite of "sending positive energy". If, on the other hand, you've experienced a surge of ideas and mental clarity while speaking, then you have experienced the potential of "sending positive energy" to others.

Before you can send it to others, you must first cultivate energy within yourself. I am not referring to adrenaline energy, but rather to a type of energy that is most noticeable by the presence of heightened mental clarity in the group participants. Personally, sending positive energy involves concentrating my attention on a person's strengths, coupled with faith in their abilities. Most of us can tell at a gut level when someone truly believes we can do something, or that we are a basically a good person. Redfield believes that loving and energizing others is one of the best things we can do for ourselves—the more support we give others, the more energy flows into us.

The topic of employing positive energy will be expanded upon later in this chapter.

"I have noticed a good many phenomena of mind disturbances that I have never been able to explain. For instance, there is the inspiration or the discouragement that a speaker feels in addressing an audience. I have experienced this many times in my life and have never been able to define exactly the physical causes of it."[3]

— *Dr. Alexander Graham Bell*

APPLICATIONS

The five primary ways I use dialogue to produce synergy in knowledge work are: strategic alliances, technology alliances, professional development alliances, public speaking opportunities, and multifunctional project teams.

STRATEGIC ALLIANCES

"Producers do it. Managers manage it. Leaders decide what 'it' is," teaches Stephen Covey. Leaders use strategic alliances to formulate overall direction and guide project selection. A board of directors is an obvious example of a strategic alliance. I've also seen CEO's of similar sized businesses in non-competing industries meet monthly to review each other's operations. Each month the focus is placed on just one

---

[3] From *Law of Success*", by Napoleon Hill.

business, which is a great way of pooling executive knowledge. Startup companies can mastermind with their investors or other partners. Participants in this type of alliance should be selected with extreme care. Additionally, it is usually not wise to discuss strategies developed by this alliance with people outside the alliance.

"Once you have seen the power inherent in human alignment, you cannot think about the future in old terms."

— Marilyn Ferguson

TECHNOLOGY ALLIANCES

Your effectiveness at implementing technology can be enhanced by building a network of individuals who have developed specialized capacity in areas complementary to your own. Developing a high degree of specialized knowledge and skill in your own niche area allows you to offer value back to your developing network. Local trade associations, national trade shows, and people you meet while working on projects are good sources of technology contacts. E-mail is a great way to interact with technical contacts because it minimizes the impact on their schedule for an information exchange event. Remember that anyone you want to talk to is usually no more than five layers of contacts away.

PROFESSIONAL DEVELOPMENT ALLIANCES

You can accelerate your efforts in assimilating and applying self-development knowledge, by finding one or more people who share your love of learning, and meet with them periodically for collaboration on self-development issues. Toastmasters International is a great way to do this. There are thousands of Toastmasters groups worldwide which meet weekly to help people develop public speaking and communication skills. In Toastmasters, you can give short speeches about self-development topics that you most want to learn. This way, you are developing a valuable skill at the same time you are helping others, acquiring knowledge about interesting new topics, and meeting high quality people who share your love of learning.

I've also found executive tape sharing clubs highly useful. This is where you get a group of people together to contribute a certain amount of money for the purchase of educational audiotapes from companies such as Nightengale-Conant (1-800-323-3938). You can get a substantial discount by purchasing ten cassette albums at a time, which can then be circulated among club members. It was through one of these clubs that I first learned of Anthony Robbins, who opened the doors to so much of the material presented in this book. The process went like this: Listen to tapes, buy book, buy books referred to in book, buy books referred to in these books, attend seminar, meet people who refer me to other quality books, tapes and seminars, which then lead to further sources of useful information.

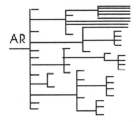

PUBLIC SPEAKING OPPORTUNITIES

While speaking before a group, we often receive positive energy from a lot of people simultaneously. As mentioned earlier, this is a great opportunity to observe the impact this energy has on your thinking. This increased awareness can help you utilize mastermind energy on various levels in other types of dialogue.

MULTIFUNCTIONAL PROJECT TEAMS

Most of this chapter discusses how to apply synergistic dialogue within multifunctional project teams. While not an authority on the design of multifunction project teams, I have been a participant in such teams with dozens of companies in a variety of industries over the past 14 years. After giving you an overview of team formation guidelines recommended in other literature, I devote the last half of the chapter towards helping individuals participate in such teams more effectively.

> *"If there is a single visible element that distinguishes [Fast Cycle Time] competitors from others, it is their extensive use of multifunctional teams."*
>
> — *Chris Myers*

In his book, *Fast Cycle Time: How to Align Purpose, Strategy, and Structure for Speed,* Christopher Meyer states that multifunctional teams "...establish the structure that brings the necessary people, regardless of technical expertise or functional base, into real-time contact to accelerate the speed of learning."

One of the most surprising lessons I learned from consulting with dozens of businesses is the degree of diversity between companies and even departments. Diversity not only in the type of problems, but in the way even common problems are addressed. While the specific requirements of project teams will vary widely, the following guidelines on project team formation seem fairly generic:

- Balance "What" and "How" Specialties. One or more people, including the project leader, must understand exactly what the customer needs. Additionally, they must know exactly how the project fits into the larger scheme of things in their business and to some extent, the industry. The other half of the team addresses the "how" part of the equation. Their job is to understand available technology and figure out the best way to apply it within agreed upon time frames to successfully complete the project. "How" people usually must be very detail oriented, especially when dealing with technology. "What" people must be adept at seeing the big picture.

- Give each person a stake in the success of the project. Give them a sense of "ownership" of their piece. One way to do this is by nurturing a sense of accountability among team members.

- Structure the work to minimize the extent to which each individual must rely on someone else for the success of their contribution.
- Create a culture that encourages clarity, efficiency, participation, commitment, and team spirit. The ideal culture is one that supports the efforts of individual team members to make their unique strengths productive.
- Use small, cohesive teams staffed with self-motivated, highly experienced, technically knowledgeable leaders. Limiting the size of each team to between three and seven people helps maintain focus.
- Weekly status meetings lay the groundwork for more focused brainstorming later on. They do this by keeping team members informed and building a sense of team— an awareness of how each person is contributing their particular skills and knowledge to the project. Consistency is a plus: same day of the week, same time, same place, same structure. The quicker the better. Just get the issues out on the table and make it clear who "owns" them. Beginning each meeting with individual "check-in" is a great way to build team synergy. This is where each member gives a brief status report on their area of the project.

TEAM SELECTION GUIDELINES

Notice individuals with whom ideas seem to flow best. Some people just take more time to build rapport with. Then there are people with whom dialogue was just not meant to be. On his *Five Keys to Wealth and Happiness* audiotape[4], Anthony

---

[4] This audiotape can be purchased by calling Robbins Research International at (800) 445-8183. It is included along

Robbins shares a related story. A speaker asks a group of kids what would happen to him if his worst enemy came along and dropped two lumps of sugar in his coffee. "Nothing" responded the children. The speaker then asked what would happen if his best friend accidentally dropped a single drop of strychnine in his coffee. "You're dead." the children replied. 'That's right," continued the teacher, "In life, your mind is like your coffee. You need to be very careful about who dumps what inside of it."

In his book *Law of Success*, Napoleon Hill writes, "It is a fact as well known to the layman as to the man of scientific investigation, that some minds clash the moment they come in contact with each other, while other minds show a natural affinity for each other." Tom Peters refers to this notion in his book, *Liberation Management*: "Jack walks into a room and 5, 55, or 555 people tense up instantly. Gloom and doom follow in his wake. Then there's Maria. She walks in, under exactly the same conditions (good or bad), and people lighten up a bit, feel a little more energetic. Look for 'Marias.' Avoid 'Jacks' like the plague."

Two more points to consider:

- Fast-paced dialogue is usually more productive.
  Visually oriented people talk faster, and this allows for higher bandwidth conversations. Anybody can develop the ability, or flexibility, to switch into a visual mode for such a conversation.

- The more team members that understand the principle of dialogue and are open to the potential for synergistic dialogue, the better. Companies who can work this material into an employee's orientation training will be at an advantage.

---

with the *Unleash the Power Within: An Owners Manual to the Brain* videotape program.

For more information on how to design a company to make use of project teams and how to design the teams themselves, refer to the following sources.

- *Fast Cycle Time: How to Align Purpose, Strategy, and Structure for Speed*, by Christopher Meyer is loaded with useful information on structuring an organization to make maximum use of project teams.
- Tom Peters' book, *Liberation Management*, discusses the dynamics of project teams at professional service firms in Chapters 11-14.
- For guidelines on structuring software development project teams, refer to Chapter 4 of the *Building Client/Server Applications with Visual Basic* manual included in the Enterprise Edition of Visual Basic 4.0.
- For information on how Microsoft uses project teams, see *Microsoft Secrets* by Michael Cusumano and Richard Selby.

The remainder of this chapter is designed to help individuals obtain maximum benefits from their participation in project teams.

GUIDELINES FOR PROJECT TEAM INTERACTION

You don't need a roomful of people to create synergistic dialogue. I derive most of the benefits of this distinction from one-on-one "hallway" or "stand-up" meetings. Such meetings are initiated by asking a project team member if they have time to "brainstorm an issue". Another useful phrase for creating the proper frame of mind for the meeting is, "Can I bounce some ideas off you?" These meetings can be done in person or over the phone. I begin the conversation by stating the issue, and then describe the challenges I am facing or the options I am considering. Oftentimes, ideas will pop into my mind without the other person even saying a word. I sometimes blurt out bizarre ideas that end up being totally useless. Not that I get a kick out of making crazy suggestions,

I just say whatever idea comes to me during the conversations that bears even the slightest relation to the issues at hand. Lousy ideas are often stepping stones to useful ones.

I don't participate in these sessions with any conscious strategy for structuring the conversation. My focus is entirely on the successful resolution of the issue. I am not trying to impress anybody with my brilliance nor am I concerned about being judged incompetent by what I say. I define a "win" on a larger scale—successful completion of the project. I know if that is accomplished, it is worth appearing foolish a time or two along the way.

The mental process I use during these one-on-one brainstorming sessions is similar to "uptime", as described by Richard Bandler and John Grinder in their book, *Frogs into Princes*. They state that you need three things to be an effective communicator: the first is to know what outcome you want, the second is that you need flexibility in your behavior—you need to be able to generate lots of different behaviors to find out what responses you get, and lastly, you need enough sensory experience to notice when you get the responses you want.

Sensory acuity is enhanced by putting themselves in "uptime". This involves operating completely in sensory experience and tuning out any awareness of internal feelings, pictures or voices. While in "uptime", all attention is directed toward how the audience is responding. These queues inspire flexible responses that help get the point across. They don't comment on the audience responses internally. They just "notice" them and adjust their behavior accordingly.

My "mastermind on the fly" strategy differs in that the objective is not to communicate something to the other person or generate a behavior, but rather to brainstorm an issue. I use all forms of the other person's reactions, verbal and nonverbal, as sources of input. My sensory acuity is tuned in to the flow of ideas into my head, whether or not they resolve the issue I am addressing. The flexibility comes in asking thought-provoking questions, or just by starting to talk about partial answers that seem promising. By talking out a partial answer, the flow of ideas seems to evolve dynamically.

I'm not claiming to have a unique gift in this area. The gift is just having an awareness of the potential and then being open to it. There have been times where I'm in a meeting with two client representatives, when all of the sudden, one of them will ask me to stand by for just a moment. The next thing I know they are having a conversation in what sounds like English—the individual words don't even seem that complicated. All I know is that I haven't the foggiest idea what they are saying. It's like I'm not tuned-in to their wavelength. They might as well be speaking Chinese.

I think what happens is that as two or more people work on a project for a while, the project itself develops its own language based upon key terminology, acronyms and metaphors. Shared experiences can be referenced by a simple word or two. This "project language" allows team members to communicate at higher bandwidths—where meaning is conveyed very rapidly with just a few words. Oftentimes, team members don't even have to complete their sentences— the others can anticipate what they are going to say.

It may be that the great results I've realized from these "stand-up" meetings stems from the fact that I've had the good fortune to work with a lot of bright people over the years. After working with hundreds of team members on dozens of projects, it is my opinion that this one-to-one or many-to-many synergy is something anyone can achieve. The process works better with some people than others. Here are some of the factors that I think contribute to synergistic dialogue:

- **Intelligence**: Some people are inherently brighter than others. Some are just better at expressing their intelligence in conversation.
- **Rapport**: Sometimes I don't get along with people— they can be the brightest person in the world, but if they don't like me to the point where they won't engage

in the conversation, the ideas just don't flow. (See discussion on "rapport" later in this section.)

- **Emotional Commitment**: The degree to which the team members care about successfully completing the project has a huge impact on dialogue effectiveness.

- **Shared Knowledge**: This is where groupware such as electronic mail can play a significant role. The better informed the participants are, the stronger the underlying foundation for high-bandwidth conversations. E-mail increases the information metabolism of the team by reducing the overhead of an information exchange event. Okay, I'll say that in English: The less time and effort it takes to exchange information, the more likely you are to do it. E-mail is discussed further in Chapter 7.

A similar phenomena occurs with larger groups, but there are some disadvantages:

- The brainstorming sessions I'm talking about usually last between one and five minutes. If you try to include more, it will take longer than that just to get them all together.

- One-on-one conversations can occur at higher bandwidths because there is only one communication style to match. The more people involved, the greater the chances that you will have to stop and explain an issue to someone who may be working on multiple projects and thus isn't quite up to speed. You may be asking, "But don't you have access to more ideas if more people are involved?" Yes, sometimes, but I seem to be able to resolve most issues just by talking things out with one individual. In some cases, I may do multiple stand-up meetings, which are often preferable to coordinating a large formal meeting. On the other hand, if the issue impacts multiple areas "owned" by multiple people, then they should have the chance to get their two cents worth in. Sometimes this can be handled by firing off an e-mail that lets them know which direction you are going, so they can respond if they disapprove.

"Don't you interrupt people a lot with this method?" I try to minimize the number of these meetings by:

- Saving up the issues for a later conversation. Sometimes I'll figure things out after my unconscious has cranked on it a while.

- Making extra effort to resolve the issue on my own. Dialogue is not an excuse to avoid having to think through an issue. You must balance dialogue with individual analysis and reasoning.

- I use e-mail as much as possible. However, I do not experience the "stepped-up" rate of thinking phenomena (nuclear beta) when writing or reading e-mail. Some issues need the energy of a dynamic conversation. If I can reduce the issue to a single clear cut question, then I use e-mail. The importance of the issue is also a factor. Deciding between e-mail and dialogue is sometimes a tough call.

- When I do ask to do a stand-up meeting, I show respect for their time by keeping the conversation as short as possible.

In knowledge work, where one is often dealing in the realm of thought, pursuing a wrong direction can be costly in both time and money. So when I sense that I'm at a critical juncture in my decision-making processes, it is usually a good time for a quick discussion. Other times, I will mentally crank on an issue to the point where I feel stuck, lost in the details, and in need of fresh perspectives. In the same way new ideas often appear when I begin writing—as if my hand knew it all along—I can gain new insights on an issue by using that part of my mind involved in a conversation. The effectiveness of dialogue is further evidence that knowledge is distributed throughout the body.

Sometimes I am credited with coming up with "great ideas" when I am sure they were more a result of the process I was using (dialogue), than a product of any brilliance. There are many cases where the other person never even gets a word out! I walk in, start talking, and 30 seconds later the idea I need hits me right between the eyes. I thank them for "all their help," and walk out. So many times they respond, "But I didn't do anything!" After over 10 years of this, I can say with a high level of certainty that they *did* a great deal. These "great ideas" were not my ideas! They were *our* ideas!

RAPPORT

My favorite strategy for building rapport is to consistently demonstrate a strong commitment to successfully completing the project. There are two dimensions to commitment: creating the appearance of commitment and the real thing— truly being committed (i.e., consistently doing the things that someone with a strong commitment would do). I try to focus on the "doing" and not worry about the appearance issue.

"When your work speaks for itself, don't interrupt."

— Bits and Pieces Magazine

When things aren't going so well, I try to remember that every disagreement or challenging relationship is a chance to learn something. I seek first to understand them, as described in Stephen Covey's *7 Habits* teachings. While listening, I send them positive energy to help them verbalize their issues. The "control drama" distinctions in *The Celestine Prophecy* are sometimes helpful in my attempts to understand them. Also helpful are the ideas in Chapters 13-15 of Anthony Robbins' book, *Unlimited Power*. These chapters are a great overview of how Neuro Linguistic Programming (NLP) distinctions can be applied to relationships. Dale Carnegie's *How to Win Friends & Influence People*, which has sold over 15 million copies, is also worth a look.

As much as possible, I emotionally disconnect from ideas presented by myself or others—they are the means. Instead I focus on the end—resolving the issue in a way that contributes to a successful project. It is usually obvious to all participants when this has been achieved. If not, then it's time to apply Stephen Covey's rule: "Value the differences," and work together to create a third alternative that satisfies both.

BUILDING POSITIVE ENERGY

When I picked up James Redfield's book, *The Celestine Prophecy*, I didn't expect to learn a distinction that would positively impact almost every discussion with another person from that point on, but that is exactly what happened. The idea was this: people have the ability to project energy consciously during a conversation.

Redfield describes the phenomena as a "conscious conversation", whereby each person speaks when the energy moves to him or her. He states that during a discussion, only one person will have the most powerful idea at any given moment. Alert participants can feel who is about to speak, and consciously focus their energy on this person, helping to bring out his or her idea with the greatest clarity. Redfield states, "The key to this process is to speak up only when it is your moment and to project energy when it is someone else's time." Quakers apply this distinction by remaining silent until they "quake" from the need to express an idea.

This process can be disrupted if a participant experiences ego inflation when in a group. This occurs when an individual gets caught up in the power of an idea. Because the burst of energy feels so good when the idea is expressed, they keep on talking long after the energy should have shifted to someone else. These individuals try to monopolize the group, causing others to pull back to the point where they won't risk expressing themselves when they feel the power of an idea. The group fragments and members don't get the benefit of all the messages. Redfield states that the same thing happens when some participants are not accepted by other members. These rejected individuals don't receive supporting energy, increasing the likelihood that the group will miss the benefit of their ideas.

This is not codependency, says Redfield, because real projection of energy has no attachment or intention, each person is just waiting for messages.

Others do not have to be aware of this principle in order to benefit from the energy you are sending them. You build positive energy within yourself by appreciating beauty and abundance in nature or life, and you project it to others by seeing them in their most positive light. Sending positive energy is the opposite of throwing mental darts, or listening with a cynical attitude.

DIALOGUE CONTRASTED WITH "CHITCHAT"

Not all conversations are created equal. The synergistic dialogue I'm referring to is directed at solving a specific problem or resolving an issue as effectively and efficiently as possible. Ben Franklin lived his life by forming the "habitude" of thirteen virtues. The second virtue was to avoid trifling conversation by only speaking words that may benefit others or himself. To quote from his autobiography: "...my desire being to gain Knowledge at the same time that I improved in Virtue, and considering that in Conversation it was obtain'd rather by the Use of the Ears than of the Tongue, & therefore wishing to break a Habit I was getting into of Prattling, Punning and Joking, which only made me acceptable to trifling Company, I gave *Silence* the second Place."

PRECISION COMMUNICATION VIA "FLUFF BUSTING" LANGUAGE

→   NLP teaches a "metamodel" for reducing language to a highly specific, sensory-based description of what another person has said. It is based on the fact that people use three basic mechanisms for creating mental models or maps of external reality. When you run out of options in a discussion, it may be time to scrub off your mental models with the following set of distinctions:

- **Generalization**: "If something is true in one case, it is probably true in other cases." The words "Always" and "Never" indicate that a person is generalizing. Bandler and Grinder point out that the ability to generalize is an essential coping skill. However, each generalization must be evaluated in its context. We limit ourselves when generalizations used in one area of our lives are transferred over to other areas where they don't apply. Sometimes it is useful to reply to such generalizations with questions such as "Always?" or "Never?"

- **Deletion**: External reality presents us with so much sensory information that we delete or ignore parts of it in order to maintain our sanity. The problem comes in when we delete information that could be used to expand our options—our behavioral flexibility. If you feel that you have run out of options in a conversation, try asking some innovative questions. When you hear the words "can't", "have to" or "should", respond with questions such as "What would happen if..?" or, "What has to happen in order for...?" Questions are a great way to open up our awareness to information we have been deleting. In his book, *Awaken the Giant Within*, Anthony Robbins teaches that asking better questions often leads to better answers. He writes that we can tear down barriers in our life by questioning our limitations—that all human progress is preceded by new questions.

- **Distortion**: Another way people distort reality is by seeing a process as an event. The statement: "That person is intelligent," is *event* language, whereas: "That person does intelligent things," is *process* language. The statement: "I don't know how to do that," is *event* language, whereas: "I don't know how to do that yet," is *process* language. One application of this distinction is that once you are aware that something is a process rather than an event, you can ask the question, "How can that process be optimized in order to better meet our objectives?"

THE SIX THINKING HATS

→ In his book *The Six Thinking Hats*, Edward de Bono has developed a communication strategy based on the use of six different colored hats to represent various complementary modes of thinking. It allows you to ask for someone's response in a particular mode of thinking just by referring to the hat color. This strategy makes it more efficient to refer the structural aspects of the conversation, which frees up more attention span for content issues. The six thinking hats help unscramble mental activity by using only one thinking mode at a time. de Bono uses the four color printing analogy: colors are printed separately in layers. When the process is complete they all come together.

He has divided these six thinking modes into three pairs of opposites:

White and Red: White is neutral and objective (just the facts please), while red is emotional (gut reactions).

Black and Yellow: While wearing the black hat, one plays the devil's advocate, looking for what's wrong. This is complemented by yellow hat thinking, which is optimistic, positive, and focuses on the potential of the ideas.

Green and Blue: The green hat is for being creative and generating new ideas, while the blue hat is concerned with control and organization—making sure that the other hats are used effectively.

If you invest the effort ahead of time to explain the simple metaphor to your teammates, then you are much better prepared to deal with an individual who is being overly pessimistic or emotional. This allows you to say things like:

"How about if we set down our red hats for a moment and emphasize what we know to be true before getting into gut reactions?"

SOWING AND REAPING IDEAS

Your efforts at communicating your desired end to your subconscious mind as described in Chapter 3, are analogous to sowing seeds. Dialogue is one of the main places where you reap the idea harvest. The more you have "primed" your "subconscious idea pump" by clearly self-communicating your desired project outcome, the more likely you are to come up with related ideas on the fly while involved in synergistic dialogue. The following factors also enhance dialogue effectiveness, and are discussed in later chapters:

- Mobilizing right-brain mental processes increases mental flexibility in conversations (Chapter 5).
- Increasing the amount of related information your mind has access to at various levels of consciousness by doing high speed scans over volumes of related information. Reviewing key terminology and concepts periodically enables faster conscious recall of these items in fast paced conversations. (Chapter 6).
- Using groupware such as e-mail to optimize the process of information sharing (Chapter 7).
- Doing things that optimize your mental clarity also increase your energy level, thus giving you access to more of your brain power (Chapter 8).

CHAPTER 5

SYNERGISTIC OSCILLATION

"Fully involve the right brain and you don't just double your brain power, you increase it many times over."

— *Colin Rose*

"The more complex the activities of the mind, the greater the need for play."

— *Star Trek*

You can achieve considerable mental leverage by oscillating between complementary modes of thinking throughout each day and on larger time scales. In addition, the mind has special requirements for rest that are not met while sleeping. This is a long chapter. It begins with a discussion of the principle of oscillation, and describes five ways of applying this distinction to enhance creativity:

- Think about an issue in a variety of states and in a variety of places. Different physiologies can be used to tune in to different sets of ideas.
- Break the creative process into complementary phases that employ different overall modes of thinking:

  1) Explore possibilities, (climb every mountain...).
  2) Analyze, rearrange, extend and reduce the ideas to form new combinations.
  3) Bring on the critical eye to decide which idea sets to act upon and in what order.

4) Switch into massive action mode and implement your ideas so that they may be tested in reality, thus providing the feedback needed to make your next attempt.

- Use mindmaps to encourage you to think about the structure of ideas and how they relate to each other—a right-brain mental process.
- Use short breaks that not only recharge, but stimulate types of thinking easily neglected in typical left-brain oriented work.
- Periodically schedule mental rest activities that rip you out of your mental ruts.

Busy readers will want to concentrate their efforts on the mindmapping section. Curious readers will want to study the principles section to understand why mindmapping is effective. Readers eager to optimize their creativity may find the "Creative Process" section to be useful.

PRINCIPLES

Consider the difference between using two legs and hopping along on one:

- It takes more energy to hop than to walk.
- The faster you need to go, the more energy hopping takes relative to walking.
- Most people can run several times faster than their top hopping speed.

Using both legs is synergistic: one plus one equals more than two. The leverage lies not in using either leg in isolation, but in using them together in harmony.

Just as we have two legs, we have two hemispheres to our brains: left and right. Nobel prize-winning researcher, Roger Sperry, has proven that each side of the brain specializes in certain activities. Yet Western society and educational systems tend to favor left-brain usage. The right-brain is capable of equally valuable yet different mental processes. Mobilizing these latent capacities has a synergistic impact on left-brain mental processes.

In Robert Ornstein's words: "It is the polarity and the integration of these two modes of consciousness, the complementary workings of the intellect and the intuitive, which underlie our highest achievements." He points out that some people have a tendency to habitually prefer one mode. Verbal, logical scientists sometimes forget or even deny that they possess another side. In such a case, they might find it difficult to do right brain activities such as art, crafts, dance, or sports. According to Ornstein, Einstein used the phrase 'combinatory play' to describe the impact these activities had on his creative thinking.

It takes discipline to override this tendency to habitually prefer one mode. Is it worth it? Consider the lives of two great thinkers in history: Albert Einstein and Leonardo da Vinci. Einstein complemented his left brain efforts in mathematics and science with violin playing, art, sailing and imagination games. da Vinci excelled in art, sculpture, physiology, architecture, mechanics, anatomy, physics, invention, meteorology, geology and engineering. The synergistic benefits of these various activities were evident in his paintings. According to Buzan, da Vinci's plans for his paintings often looked like architectural plans.

Did these two men accomplish great things because they were geniuses, and thus had the mental capacity to do these complimentary activities? Or did performing these complimentary activities help them accomplish great things? Probably some combination of both. It is more useful to emphasize the latter—"Smart is as smart does," to paraphrase Forrest Gump.

TIPPING THE FIRST DOMINO

➜   So how does one "tip the first domino" in breaking this tendency to involve only one brain hemisphere? Here are four overall strategies:

1) Give yourself a reason to do so. Set a goal for yourself or take on a project that demands the use of your latent capacities. To activate subdominant visual/perceptual right-brain processes, present your mind with a task that the analytical/verbal left-brain processes will reject.[5] The tendency for most people is not to think unless they have to. Truly committing to a challenging project that demands the use of right-brain thinking can be a booster rocket on your mental journey from "Can't" to "MUST!"

2) Decide to teach this material to others. This shifts your paradigm in a way that increases the degree to which you pay attention. It forces you to crystallize your thoughts— to organize, simplify and fine tune them. Tony Robbins makes a key point when he states that most people will do far more to help others than they'll ever do for themselves.

3) Act "as if". Begin doing an activity that requires right-brain activity acting as if you already know how to do it. As discussed later in this chapter, mindmapping is an excellent opportunity to apply this strategy.

4) Model someone. Find creative people and observe them. It is one thing to use complementary opposites and quite another to do it effectively.

OVERVIEW OF COMPLEMENTARY OPPOSITES

To some extent, the idea of oscillating between left and right hemispheric mental processes is more of a metaphor than a hard and fast rule. Much work remains to figure out exactly which part of the brain is doing what. As a knowledge worker, the important question is not *which* part of the brain is involved, but rather which thinking styles are complementary opposites and what areas have been neglected that offer the potential for mental leverage. Figure 5.1 summarizes the difference between left and right-brain mental processes.

---

[5] Suggested by Betty Edwards in *Drawing on the Right Side of Your Brain.*

Left-brain Mode	Right-brain Mode
Thinking in words, analyzing something in a linear, step-by-step fashion. Reducing a problem to smaller chunks. Using symbols such as 1, 2, 3 or +, -, /, and * as in mathematics. Remaining aware of time while you are doing something. Using reason and logic to make decisions based on facts.	Being aware of something without labeling it or using words to describe the experience. Seeing the big picture, how parts or ideas relate to each other and the overall context: awareness of high level structure. Synthesizing. Operating without an awareness of time: going with the flow. Thinking in metaphors to transfer meaning from one context to another. Rhythm and spatial awareness.

Figure 5.1. Left-brain vs. right-brain thought processes.[6]

Brain Dancing involves using the strengths of both modes in a way that they complement the other. For example, using the right brain as the idea factory, and the left to provide a context in which those ideas can be applied. Using left-brain mode to come up with questions, and right-brain mode to provide possible answers that the left-brain can analyze. Using the left brain to make a decision and the intuitive, wholistic right brain to do an ecology check.

While the emphasis in this chapter is on achieving right/left synergy, the notion of using complementary opposite modes of thinking goes beyond left/right synergy. Figure 5.2 elaborates on the thought spectrum chart introduced in Chapter 1. It is presented to emphasize the broad range of complementary opposite thinking styles that are possible.

---

[6] Adapted from material in Betty Edwards book, *Drawing on the Right Side of the Brain*, and *The Brain Book*, by Peter Russell

Scale	Range of Thought
Focus	**Daydreaming vs. Concentrated**. Daydreaming, or just letting your mind wander where it will, is facilitated by looking off in the distance or defocusing your eyes. Concentration is grabbing your "mental reins" and directing your thoughts toward achieving a specific end.
Awareness	**Subconscious vs. Conscious**. If consciousness were an ocean, some thoughts occur deep down where there isn't much light of awareness and others occur at the surface level. A person can have feelings about something deep down that they are not fully aware of. They can also be saying things to themselves or picturing things that they don't realize.
Time Orientation	**Past vs. Present vs. Future**. We can think about things that have already happened, things that are happening right now, and things that we would like to happen in the future. This is called your "timeline". You can make any one of these your *modus operandi*. "He's living in the past" or "She's acting as if it has already happened." You can also change the way you think about each of these. You can think of your future as bright or dim.
Decision	**Minor vs. Destiny Shaping**. Contrast the relative importance of deciding who to marry with what you will wear today. The important thing is selecting the appropriate decision-making strategy for each level of decision.
Inquiry	**Questions vs. Answers**. Asking better questions often results in better answers. A good question to ask is: "How will I recognize a great answer when I see it?" Then keep asking questions until you come up with an answer that meets those criteria.
Modality	**Kinesthetic vs. Auditory vs. Visual**. When thinking about an issue, we can consider how we feel about it, what our conscience tells us in words, and what pictures come to mind when we think about it.

Attitude	**Positive vs. Negative.** Faith, hope and love are the emotional opposites of fear, despair and hatred. Negative attitudes are best avoided or used with extreme caution.
Emotion	**Passionate vs. Ambivalent.** The degree of emotional attachment to or personal investment in an issue impacts the nature of the thoughts that occur to us on that issue. Contrast a "burning desire" with an "I could care less" attitude.
Brain Wave Frequency	**Delta->Theta->Alpha->Beta.** The mind generates different brain waves depending on the mode of consciousness as discussed in Chapter 3.
Dialogue	**None vs. Two or More People.** Something special happens to our thinking processes when discussing an issue with others who share our concern for its resolution.
Detail Level	**General vs. Specific.** Read an encyclopedia and then read a computer software manual. This spectrum deals with the level of information at which we are focusing our conscious resources.

Figure 5.2. Thought Spectrum Chart Revisited.

In his book, *Using Both Sides of Your Brain*, Tony Buzan writes that developing a mental area previously considered weak, rather than detracting from other areas, seems to produce a synergistic effect in which other areas of mental performance are improved. When I find an activity that requires a huge amount of discipline to perform or even attempt, that is often a sign that I'm about to create some intrapersonal synergy.

The next section looks at how some very creative people apply the principle of oscillation.

THE CREATIVE PROCESS

Edison took short naps, Einstein played the violin, da Vinci engineered his paintings. Japanese inventor, Yoshiro

NakaMats, uses a three-step oscillation process, creativity consultant, Roger von Oech, suggests alternating between four complementary opposite roles, and, as discussed in Chapter 4, Dr. Edward de Bono teaches six "Thinking Hats" which correspond to three pairs of opposite thinking styles. This section explores strategies used by some highly creative people.

THE BEST OF THE BEST

→ Have you ever wondered who invented compact disks, floppy disks, and digital watches? The answer is Dr. Yoshiro NakaMats, a Japanese inventor who holds over 2,300 patents (Edison had 1,093) and has won the grand prize at the International Exposition of Inventors in New York City for seven years running.

In his excellent book, *What a Great Idea*, Charles Thompson interviewed Dr. NakaMats to better understand the sccrets to his extraordinary success. Each of the three steps in Dr. NakaMats creative process is done in a separate room.

- **Static Room:** In this room, Dr. NakaMats calms himself as much as possible. It is a place of peace and quiet filled with natural things such as a rock garden, natural running water and plants. The walls are white and he can look out over the Tokyo skyline, but the room contains no metal or concrete. He uses this room to free-associate, letting his mind wonder where it will––just the opposite of meditating. Before focusing on one thing in the next room, the static room is used to churn out volumes of ideas.

- **Dynamic Room:** The dynamic room is the opposite of the static room. This dark room has black and white striped walls and leather furniture. He starts out listening to jazz, shifts to easy listening, and always finishes up with Beethoven's Fifth Symphony. Using such opposite decor may serve as an environmental anchor for conditioning his thinking to switch modes as he moves between rooms.

- **Creative Swimming Room:** The final step in the process involves holding his breath in a special way and swimming underwater with a plexiglas writing pad. It is here that he comes up with his best ideas. According to Lynn Schroeder and Sheila Ostrander in their book, *Superlearning 2000*, Dr. NakaMats sits cross-legged on the bottom in five feet of water in four to five minute stretches. "The water pressure forces blood and oxygen into my brain, making it work at peak performance," NakaMats explains.

Schroeder and Ostrander report that Dr. NakaMats is now a billionaire.

Similarly, Walt Disney overcame the impact criticism has on creative, original thinking by sequencing his creative process into three functional stages: "Dreamer", "Realist", and "Critic". Each function was carried out in a different room.[7]

Roger von Oech believes one of the reasons we forget is that our memory is state bound. Changing our state changes the associations we "notice" in our mind. The most obvious example of this phenomena goes something like this: while sitting on the couch in the living room, you realize that you need something from the bedroom. When you get to the bedroom, you have no idea what you went in there for, so you head back. As soon as your rear hits the couch, you remember what it was.

Not only is our memory state bound, but so is our thinking. Dr. de Bono believes that the six thinking hats can eventually develop into anchors for triggering specific chemical backgrounds in the brain which support the different modes of thinking.

---

[7] For a detailed analysis of the mental proceses Walt Disney used in his creative thinking, refer to *Skills for the Future*, by NLP pioneer Robert Dilts. (408) 464-0254.

Ever wonder why you get ideas when you are flying in an airplane? It may have something to do with the fact that your physiology is different in a pressurized cabinet at 35,000 feet. It may also have something to do with the notion put forth by Alexander Graham Bell, that various thoughts are bouncing around in the ether along with radio and television waves. Traveling through the heavens at high speeds may increase the diversity of thoughts you travel through.

Effective creativity involves the synthesis of complementary processes and phases. The lesson is this: when involved in creative problem solving, vary your physiology and think about the issue in different locations. Dr. NakaMats seems to apply this principle to the nth degree. While trying to generate new ideas while working at a client, I sometimes apply this principle by walking up a hill where I can look out over a distance. Other times I take a pad or pencil to the cafeteria, library or even a conference room. These rooms seem to trigger different "modes of thinking" and broaden my access to ideas.

This link between state and idea flow may also explain why we get so many ideas while taking showers. Next time you shower, notice all of the unique movements involved in scrubbing down. If you get ideas when you shower, one teacher suggested taking more showers when you want more ideas. I guess a person could apply this at work by standing up in their office and begin moving around as if they were taking a shower. Imagine having to explain that to your boss: "Well, uh, I was just Brain Dancing in an attempt to create a shower of innovative ideas into my mind."

Dr. NakaMats suggests that we can improve the flow of ideas into our mind by eating only the best foods and avoiding alcohol. Food can have a dramatic impact on our state; positive or negative. This topic is explored in depth in Chapter 8—Optimizing Mental Clarity.

ROGER VON OECH'S FOUR ROLES FOR HIGHLY CREATIVE PERFORMANCE

➔   In his book, *A Kick in the Seat of the Pants*, Roger von Oech recommends alternating between four roles—Explorer, Artist, Judge, and Warrior—for highly creative performance.

Explorer: This mode involves gathering the raw materials from which ideas can be made. Ideas such as facts, theories, rules, concepts, feelings, and impressions. In this role, the high speed scanning skills discussed in Chapter 6 are invaluable. von Oech suggests that you do whatever it takes to break out of your mental ruts and routines and come to grips with the possibility that you may discover something that profoundly impacts your life. He recommends that you temporarily set aside your need to specialize—to be a master of a narrow field which is often so valuable to businesses. I believe that the principle of "personal ecology" plays a significant role in buying yourself this flexibility. If you are going to abandon your structure, you had better do it in a structured way—by setting specific time limits on your unstructured time. I use the Explorer mode by periodically visiting bookstores, libraries, trade shows, or surfing the Internet. These sources provide so much information, that if I don't set specific time limits, I might get carried away and end up spending more time than I can really afford. So the price for giving myself the freedom to explore these vast information storehouses is the discipline it takes to set a specific time limit for this exploration and then sticking to it.

Artist: After you broaden your idea pool on a given subject, von Oech suggests that you perform a variety of mental gymnastics to do something to your information. He suggests asking what patterns you can change and how you can alter the way you think about an issue. von Oech gives several suggestions for using imagination to transform raw information into useful ideas while in this mode. Mindmaps, as discussed in the next section, are a useful tool for operating in this mode.

Judge: Evaluate an idea and decide what to do with it: implement, modify, or discard. von Oech says this is the role people are most likely to get stuck in. The judge neither creates nor implements, so if you spend too much time in this role you risk not getting much accomplished. I use this mode when converting mindmapped ideas into linear plans for action, whether that plan be the precise order to deliver a speech, write a paper, or accomplish a task.

Warrior: In this role you carry your ideas from the world of "what if" into the world of action. von Oech suggests that the creative process is not a series of linear steps, but an ongoing cycle. The warrior completes the loop thus providing feedback to the other roles. Schedule your most productive time for warrior mode activities.

The next three sections will give you three specific techniques that bridge the gap between oscillation theory and practical application:

- **Mindmaps:** Outlines a three-step process for using mindmapping and related techniques to optimize the creative writing process.
- **5-10 minute breaks:** Sometimes the most productive thing you can do when performing a challenging task is take a short break. This section suggests some of the most effective break activities I've discovered.
- **Mental Rest:** On a larger scale, the mind needs to rest just as the body does, yet the mind does not rest while we sleep. This section discusses the principle and strategies for achieving effective mental rest.

MINDMAPS

Mindmaps were invented by Tony Buzan in the 1960's while he was serving as editor for the *International MENSA Journal*. Buzan introduced this technique in his book, *Using Both Sides of the Brain*, and recently published an update called *The Mind Map Book*. This latest book is now the definitive work on the subject.

Mindmaps give you a new way to represent ideas on paper that more closely resembles how ideas are stored in your mind. The technique is so different from established norms, that it has met some cultural resistance. However, mindmaps are beginning to make inroads into mainstream business. For example, Buzan's latest book mentions that Boeing condensed an engineering manual into a 25-foot long mindmap. This enabled a team of 100 senior aeronautical engineers to learn in a few weeks what had previously taken a few years. The result was an estimated savings of $11 million.

Figure 5.3 is a mindmap of the content of this chapter. Notice how concisely it conveys the structure of the ideas.

When I list the rules for mindmap creation later in this chapter, you will notice that I don't always follow them. For myself, mindmaps usually serve as a means to an end, not an end in themselves, and I adapt them accordingly. For example, Figure 5.3 is intended to convey structural information about this chapter to first time readers. Therefore, it includes a few extra words that I would not have used if it were intended exclusively for my own use.

Four years passed between the time I first learned of mindmaps and when I actually started using them. I remember being sort of proud that I even knew what they were. Taking so long to bridge the gap between "knowing" and "doing" was a mistake. The following material is designed to help shorten your journey from awareness to actual use.

What I've discovered is that mindmaps are much more than another note taking method. In addition to increasing my understanding of how my mind works, they have improved my memory, creative thinking, writing skills, and reading effectiveness. The process of learning to draw is a great way to learn how your brain handles information.

Many accelerated learning strategies involve techniques which mobilize both hemispheres of the mind in a synergistic fashion. Mindmapping does this by helping you think at "meta" levels—dealing with the structure of information and seeing how the ideas relate to each other—a right-brain mental process. Sometimes the essence is in how the ideas relate to each other. Mindmaps encourage creative leaps and new associations.

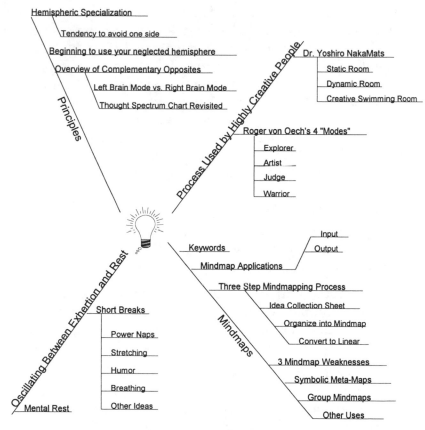

Figure 5.3. Chapter 5 mindmap drawn with Visio software.

The easiest way to get started using mindmaps is to just start doing them "as if" you already know how. Set short time limits on your initial efforts (5-10 minutes) so you don't get carried away. Periodically refer to the rules in order to gradually refine your technique. I have found value in even the most rule-breaking of mindmaps. As mentioned earlier, most mindmaps I create are means, not ends—they are just a step in the process of getting the work done, and are often discarded when the task is done or even before.

While mindmaps involve using pictures, it is not usually a wise investment of your time to make them works of art. Quick sketches often serve just fine. That is, of course, unless you plan to publish them in a book on mindmapping or use them for training purposes. Tony Buzan's latest book presents truly awesome examples of mindmaps that are actually works of art. While this may be an excellent way to mobilize right-brain capacity, I create so many mindmaps, that to make each one a work of art would make their use impractical. I rarely use mindmaps in "Warrior" mode; this is a time for action, not tossing ideas around as in the "Artist" phase of a project.

KEYWORD CONCEPT

→   The idea of "keywords" is a fundamental concept in mindmapping and has broad implications for other mental processes. Consider the following sentence:

> While computers have come a long way and had a dramatic impact on society, the potential of multimedia and the information superhighway offer strong evidence that the computer revolution has really just begun.

The key ideas in this sentence, the words that are most memorable and contain the essence of the sentence, are *computers,* *impact* *society,* *multimedia,* *information superhighway,* and *revolution just begun.* The remaining words are merely grammatical constructions and emphasis. They are not necessary for recall. Take one of the following paragraphs and highlight the keywords, the words that represent the essence of the meaning to you, and will help you recall its content. These are the words to use on mindmaps.

In actual application, I've noticed that keywords are highly personal. First of all, some words trigger different meaning for different people. Secondly, the keywords you want to emphasize depend heavily on your specific objectives at the time. Substantive text often addresses issues from a variety of angles. Life is multidimensional, written text is linear. The keyword distinction can help you bridge this mental gap in a way that is appropriate to your circumstances.

Several chapters in this book include a mindmap of the chapter's content. The mindmaps you draw of each chapter may be completely different. Material you have already mastered needs very little attention. Other ideas may be so new that you'll want to mindmap them in much more detail. This personal aspect of keywords is one of the main reasons I feel that mindmaps are often a means and not an end.

TWO MAIN WAYS OF USING MINDMAPS

The way you use mindmaps depends on whether you are taking information in (Explorer mode) or doing something with the information (Artist and Judge modes). Since the emphasis of this chapter is creative thinking, I will emphasize the "Output" side of the mindmapping equation. The next chapter covers the "Input" side.

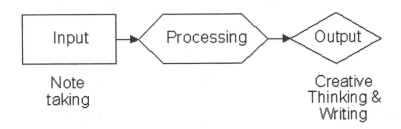

Figure 5.4 Two Basic Uses of Mindmaps.

THREE STEP MINDMAPPING PROCESS

Whether you are writing a speech, technical white paper, specification, strategic plan or a chapter in a book, the following three-step process can be applied:

1) **Idea Collection**: Use various brainstorming techniques to gather your thoughts on a specific topic.

2) **Idea Mapping**: Create mindmaps that organize your thoughts structurally.

3) **Conversion to Linear form**: When writing or speaking, ideas must be presented one word after another. The challenge is to present the material in a way that the associations and structure of the material are not lost.

These are general guidelines to be adapted to specific circumstances. For example, when doing presentations, I'll sometimes do step 3 "on the fly", trusting my subconscious to pull the material off the mindmap spontaneously.

IDEA COLLECTION SHEETS

➜ Idea collection sheets serve as a bridge across the space and time that separate the great ideas you are capable of coming up with on any specific topic. The steps are:

1) Use unlined paper. Lined paper shuts down the right brain. I use 11x17 or larger paper when tackling major issues.

2) Try turning the paper sideways. "Landscape" mode seems to work better for me in part because it helps me see more of the page at one time.

3) Write the topic in the center and circle it, or quickly sketch a symbol representing the essence or theme of what you plan to write.

4) Set your stopwatch for 5-7 minutes, or just jot the ending time in the upper left corner as a reminder.

5) As quickly as possible, write as many ideas related to this topic as you can. Use personal shorthand, abbreviations,

symbols you've developed, or any other method you have for writing at higher bandwidths. This is not a steadfast rule. To evolve an idea, I sometimes choose to write a short sentence. Collecting ideas is an art, not a science. Your success is measured by the quality of the ideas you come up with, and not by how many of the rules you followed in coming up with them. Use whatever writing instrument allows you to write the fastest in the most comfortable manner. Avoid pens that drag across the paper unless held at a certain angle.

The idea collection phase differs from the mindmapping phase. Many of the aspects of mindmapping disrupt the rapid flow of ideas during this phase's mental burst. For example, in the idea collection phase:

- Use the same writing instrument throughout. Don't take time to switch pens to write or draw in a different color.
- Write down your ideas as they flow without judging whether the idea is related to the topic. Some ideas are "mental bridges" to other useful and more directly related ideas.
- Write your ideas in the first place that comes to mind. Don't take the time to position the idea in the optimal place. Placement is a mindmapping step.

After completing the initial mental burst, take a short break to incubate related ideas. The 5-10 Minute Break Ideas section later in this chapter offers some ideas. After your break, take 30-40 minutes to pull related ideas from various reference materials. Follow this session with another short break or just move on to another project. Some topics require multiple passes.

If possible, place the idea collection sheet in a place where it will be handy over the next day or two. When related ideas come to you, write them on this sheet, or jot them in your calendar and transfer them to the idea collection sheet when convenient. I usually carry a portfolio around which contains a few sheets of unlined paper for this purpose. Idea collection sheets in progress are often stored here or in the adjacent pocket. Carrying my idea collection sheets around with me allows me to round them out from the perspective of a variety of mental states.

CATEGORIZING IDEAS

Using idea collection sheets as a precursor to mindmapping was inspired in part by material in Charles Thompson's book, *What a Great Idea*. Thompson suggests using various symbols such as circles, squares and triangles to help categorize the points on the idea collection sheet before organizing them into a map. For example, in reviewing an idea collection sheet, you might notice that there are four main themes to the ideas. You could place a circle around all ideas related to theme one, a triangle for ideas related to theme two, etc. These symbols make it apparent how many ideas relate to each theme, which helps you decide how to organize them in the mindmap.

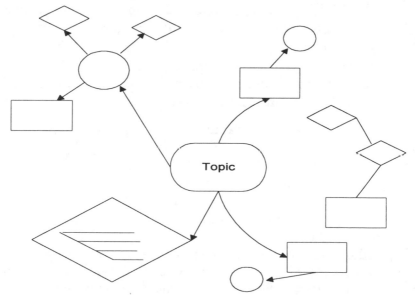

Figure 5-5. Using Symbols to Categorize Items on Idea Collection Sheets. Ideas are placed on sheet quickly without much concern for neatness or organization.

Now that you've gathered your thoughts, you are ready to organize them into a structure based on how they relate to each other. This leads us to mindmaps.

"Surveys of creative thinking have emphasized the importance of encouraging an initial right brain visualization, an intuitive solution, which can subsequently be evaluated logically by left brain processes."

— Colin Rose

CONVERTING TO MINDMAP FORM

The rules for converting ideas into a mindmap are as follows:

1) Use unlined paper or a whiteboard. Sometimes bigger paper allows "bigger thinking". One client made an entire wall into a whiteboard for strategic thinking and planning.

2) Start by drawing a color symbol in the middle of the page. This encourages right brain activity from the outset. If an image doesn't come to me in 10-15 seconds, I use keywords and circle them with a border. Sometimes the border is simply a geometric shape such as a square or circle. Other times I use shapes like a 3-D book or computer monitor. At any rate, the best way to get it done is <u>quickly</u>!

3) Branch the main ideas off this central image.

4) Use one keyword or symbol per line. Avoiding clutter permits more ideas to be represented and encourages your mind to see how they relate to each other.

5) Print the words on top of the lines. Printed words are easier to read than cursive.

6) Use color throughout. This can be especially useful in grouping related ideas.

7) Use images throughout your mindmap. In practice, I usually include a few quick sketches and symbols. But I don't think "on the job" is the best place to create a

drawing masterpiece unless they are to be used by others. Most of my mindmaps are used as means, not ends.

At this point, you know *what* you want to communicate— the substance. You still have to figure out the *how*—the sequence. Whether you are writing a paper or delivering a speech, these are linear forms of communication where the material must be presented one word at a time.

CONVERSION TO LINEAR FORM

➔   In the case of a speech, you have three possibilities: writing it out word for word (extreme left-brain approach), winging it from your mindmap (extreme right-brain approach), or something in-between. Sometimes I write out the speech based on my mindmap simply as a mental exercise, then use new distinctions gained from this writing to evolve a new more sequential mindmap organized something like Figure 5.6.

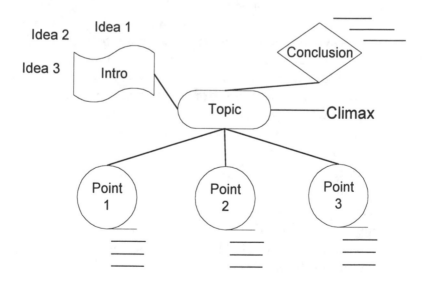

Figure 5-6. "Linear" mindmap for speech delivery.

The more right brain deliveries you rehearse from such a linear mindmap, the better your chances of "winging it" successfully in front of an audience.

THREE WEAKNESSES OF MINDMAPS

→   Mindmaps are usually not well suited for representing lots of detailed technical information. Mindmaps are gestalt thinking tools. The more detailed information represented, the more likely you are to loose sight of the forest for the trees. To compensate, I often use cross-references to indicate where I can get the details if needed.

For example, rather than clutter a mindmap with a bunch of phone numbers, I use mindmaps to diagram all the sources of information available to me for a given topic. The notes on the mindmap are enough to remind me of where I can get the information I need to act on it. Phone numbers, Internet addresses, etc. might be useful in some cases, but in others, they change the nature of the mindmap to a detail tool rather than an overview tool.

Boeing addressed this issue by using bigger paper. They created a 25 foot wide and four foot high mindmap of their "Quality/Productivity Improvement Process". The only challenge is that you can't see the entire map at a single glance and actually have to walk several steps to get from one end to the other. However, this map was highly effective for them, so it depends on your situation and objectives.

The second weakness to watch out for is that keywords are often personal in the memories they trigger. To the extent that others will be referring to your mindmaps, you must be sure to use keywords and key symbols that remind others of the same thoughts.

Lastly, the more information mindmaps contain, the harder it is to use them for reference purposes. In some cases, it gets harder to locate specific pieces of information. Finding information is helped by first locating the related main branch. In practice, I derive the most value from the process of creating mindmaps and from how they streamline the process of review. The creation itself reinforces my understanding of the material, and the review process enhances recall.

SYMBOLIC META-MAPS

➜ In writing this book, I found it extremely useful to create what I called a Symbolic Meta-Map (SMM). This involved placing nine pieces of 33" x 27" flip chart paper on a wall as represented in Figure 5-7. Each sheet represented one chapter.

My objective with the SMM was to represent as much information as possible as efficiently as possible. I wanted to symbolize ideas to the point where I could mentally traverse the content of the entire book in just a few minutes. The SMM became a tool for thinking about how the ideas would flow from chapter to chapter.

The purpose of each section was as follows:

- **Objectives**: In the lower right-hand corner of each sheet, I wrote my specific objectives for the chapter. Only ideas that contributed to these ends made it on the sheets. These objectives also helped me know when I was "done" with a chapter.

- **Chapter Symbols**: A simple symbol was selected for each chapter and placed in the upper left corner of the corresponding sheet. These symbols were used to classify lists of ideas, Daytimer journal entries, and Post-it tabs placed in books that I wanted to reference. When working on a chapter, I could pick up lots of books on the subject and quickly locate sections related to that chapter. I could also easily flip through my journal and reference just the ideas related to the chapter I was working on.

- **Sticky notes**: All ideas were placed on Post-it notes of various sizes and colors (sometimes I used normal paper with a little tape). This allowed me to easily move the ideas around on and between sheets. Different sizes and colors were used for different categories of ideas (beliefs, principles, quotes, metaphors, examples, action items, etc.)

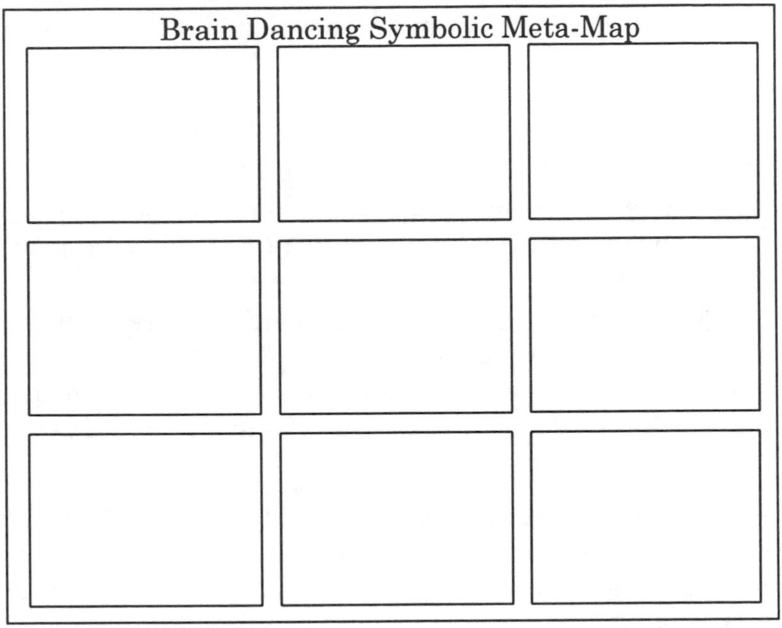

Figure 5-7. Symbolic Meta-Map Covering Entire Wall.

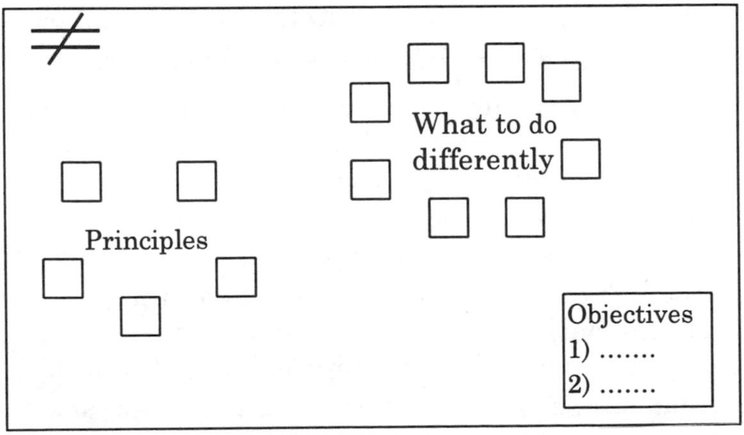

Figure 5-8. One Chapter in Symbolic Meta-Map.

- **Placement**: Initially, the ideas were just pasted randomly on the sheet corresponding to the chapter in which I thought they belonged. The ideas were then divided according to whether they described a principle or instructed the reader on what to do differently. Related ideas were stacked on top of each other. For example, this chapter's "What to do differently" section had a sticky note entitled "5-10 Minute Breaks" (discussed in the next section). Behind this note I had stacked several notes representing the different types of short breaks a person can take.
- **Cross-references**: I developed symbols for referencing material in other places. For example, "DT 4/5/94" meant "see related material in my Daytimer on April 5, 1994." "REE 64" meant "see page 64 in the book *Re-engineering the Corporation*."

In addition to helping me organize this book, this Meta-map was very helpful when it came to writing each chapter. Large complex projects are ideal candidates for using this variation of mindmapping.

THE GROUP MINDMAP

→   In *The Mind Map Book*, Tony Buzan gives the following seven-step process for creating a group mindmap:

1) Clearly define the topic and objectives. The question I like to ask is: "When we walk out of this meeting, how will we know that we were successful?"
2) Each member does an individual mindmap of the topic using the three-step process outlined earlier in this chapter.
3) In groups of three to five people, ideas from each individual mindmap are discussed and combined while each member maintains a positive and accepting attitude.
4) A group mindmap is then created on a wall-size sheet of paper or white-board combining the ideas from each

sub-group. One individual from each sub-group participates in this process.

5) Time is allowed to pass as the ideas "sink in" and incubate.

6) Steps 2, 3, and 4 are then repeated from the new perspective generated by this "incubation" period.

7) The material is then analyzed and decisions are made for specific plans of action.

Walt Disney used to post his ideas on large boards for his staff to review and note their ideas as they came to mind. In her book, *Mindmapping*, Joyce Wycoff describes a related technique she calls "brainwriting". Sheets of paper are divided into 21 squares (three across and seven down). Create one more sheet of paper than members in the group. Each person writes three ideas on a sheet and returns it to the middle and takes another sheet. This is repeated until the boxes are filled up or group runs out of ideas or energy.

Sometimes it helps to crank up your energy level with a "woo-clap" during a mindmapping session. This is a technique Anthony Robbins uses in his seminars to keep his audience energized during his 14-hour marathon presentations. Everybody stands with one hand extended out down to the left and the other up to the right. You take a full breath, shake your hands while saying "wooooooo" in a tone that gradually gets louder and louder. At a certain point, each person brings their hands together in a loud clap and says "Yyyyeeeesssss!!!!" in a fairly loud and energetic voice. Words don't do the woo-clap justice. You know you are doing them correctly when your energy level increases significantly.

OTHER MINDMAP APPLICATIONS

If you are just beginning to learn how to mindmap, then there is a reasonable chance that you don't know what you don't know. At least this was true with me. Some distinctions are best discovered by just "tipping the first domino" and start doing them. This is new territory and the last word on mindmaps has not been written. You may even discover a new, more useful way to do them.

For example, Jeff B.R. Gaspersz, Ph.D, associate professor of Human Resource Management at Nijenrode University in the Netherlands, suggests the following: Write the idea you are working on in the middle of the page and then draw six lines, one for each thinking mode represented by Dr. de Bono's six hats. Think about the issue from each perspective to see what ideas flow onto the page. Then examine them as a whole.

If you are just beginning to learn how to access the Internet, you may want to create an ongoing mindmap of what you learn. Each time you pick up a new distinction, you can add it to this sheet and see how it relates to other ideas you have discovered. The larger the body of information surrounding what you are learning, the more helpful it will be to create an ongoing mindmap.

Mindmaps and related tools play a key role in several of my knowledge work and personal activities. In the next chapter, you will see how they help optimize reading effectiveness. In Chapter 9, I discuss how I use these tools to evolve and "detect" my mission statement, values, and goals. I also use them in time management and journal writing.

2-10 MINUTE BREAKS

Oscillating between focus and rest is just as important as oscillating between right-mode and left-mode thinking. One of the most valuable things I learned in college was to take a ten-minute break every two hours. It helped me graduate two quarters ahead of my class with honors and pass the CPA exam while still in college. It worked so well that I began to ask: "What is the smartest thing I can do during this ten-minute break?" and, "What will have the greatest rejuvenating effect on my mind and body?" This is when I discovered the ten-minute power nap.

Since then I've learned that it also helps to take short breaks every 30-40 minutes. This, along with new distinctions about mobilizing right-brain mental capacity, encouraged me to develop additional turbo-charging short break ideas. This section summarizes activities that can be done quickly in an office setting to complement the intense concentration required to perform challenging knowledge work.

10 MINUTE POWER NAPS

→ When others hear that I take ten minute naps during the day, they often respond with: "I could never do that. I'd sleep for hours or feel all groggy afterwards." I'll bet at some point they couldn't ride a bicycle either. Like riding bicycles, taking power naps is a skill that must be learned. Countless times in my life, I have awakened ten minutes to the second after laying down, and felt *more* refreshed than I feel after sleeping a solid seven or eight hours at night!

John D. Rockefeller, who lived to be ninety-eight, took a half-hour nap every day at noon. Edison attributed his enormous energy and endurance to his habit of sleeping whenever he wanted to. Dale Carnegie suggested that you could add one hour per day to your waking life by sleeping six hours at night instead of eight, and then taking a one-hour nap before the evening meal. He felt that this would do you more good than eight hours of unbroken sleep.

Dr. NakaMats sleeps only four hours a night, and then takes two 30-minute naps during the day in a Cerebrex chair that he designed. He claims that an hour in his chair refreshes the brain as much as eight hours of sleep. According to Dr. NakaMats, this chair improves memory, math skills, creativity, and in some cases, lowers blood pressure, improves eyesight, and cures ailments. This is accomplished with special sound frequencies that pulse from footrest to headrest. These vibrations stimulate blood circulation and increase brain synaptic activity.

Until your company purchases a Cerebrex chair, Bio-Battery, Voyager, Mindscope or other device for getting compressed rest, here are some guidelines that might help you get started with 10-minute power naps.

1) Find a place with a comfortable temperature and very little or no noise. Noisy computer fans in the same room make effective napping impossible for me. Try to give your ears a break from the sounds they hear throughout the working day.

2) Always nap on a flat hard surface and lay flat on your back. Conference room floors work well in the winter, or outside on a bench in warmer weather. Lying on a grass lawn also works well. The surface must be as close to level as possible. One of the benefits seems to be that it momentarily removes the burden of gravity from your internal organs while equalizing and redistributing body fluids.

3) Look at your watch before closing your eyes and decide exactly when you want to wake up. I usually use the digital stop watch component of my watch, which removes any doubt about when I need to wake.

4) Cover your eyes or turn off the lights. Coat sleeves do just fine.

5) Relax your entire body as much as possible and settle in as comfortable a position as possible. I sometimes do some light stretching or a couple of "complete breaths" to help me relax. A complete breath begins by slowly inhaling through the nose to fill your lower lungs completely, then inhaling further to fill your upper lungs, holding for a few seconds and then exhaling slowly. When you exhale, you want to completely empty the lungs and begin the next breath without pausing. Complete breaths should be done comfortably without straining yourself.

6) Take naps when you need them. For me, this is usually right after lunch or right before dinner. Some people reach for caffeine when their eyes get heavy. I take a nap.

A friend interested in learning this technique studied me while I napped on several occasions. She noted that I go completely unconscious. I seem to slow my breathing and heart rate significantly, but not consciously. I just try to relax as much as possible and my body takes over from there.

"Remember also that, in most instances, diversion from one activity to another is more relaxing than complete rest...the body is not built to take too much stress always on the same part."

— *Hans Selye*

STRETCHING

Stretching improves circulation and energy flow by releasing body tension. A flexible body contributes to a flexible mind. Chapter 8 discusses several techniques and references for refining your stretching skills and discipline. The important thing to note is that stretching is best done after warming up a bit, either by going for a walk or doing some jumping jacks. I've hurt my neck twice while doing a rather intense stretch without adequate warm-up. The second time I misjudged how much warm-up I needed.

HUMOR

Dr. James E. Loehr and Peter J. McLaughlin state that humor can lower your blood pressure and pulse rate, increase the flow of blood to your brain, increase your energy level, and encourage you to take fuller breaths. Humor helps us be more creative.[8]

Humor is all around us if we only tune in. You might want to set up a joke file so that the next time you hear a good joke you can save it away for the next time you need a good laugh.

"You can always tell an intelligent person—they have the same views as you do."

— *Walt Evans*

---

[8] Adapted from their *Mental Toughness* audiotape.

If you have e-mail at work, consider setting up a humor alias. Over time, build up an electronic network of associates who value humor. When one of you discovers a humorous line or story, e-mail it to the alias coordinator. The coordinator maintains a personal group in their e-mail software containing a list of people in the humor alias. If they deem it worthy, they will forward the humorous text on to everyone in the group.

"Lord, help my words be gracious and tender today, because I may have to eat them tomorrow."

— Walt Evans

BREATHING

The brain consists of 3% of our body mass yet it consumes 20% or more of the oxygen we take in. That's a sentence worth reading again. Breathe smarter and you will think smarter. Not all breaths are created equal. If you work in an office building, try walking outside in the fresh, non-processed, non-dried out air and take a few complete breaths or alternate nostril breaths (discussed in Chapter 8). The movement of breath is said to be the movement of consciousness. It alters our physiology by altering the flow of oxygen in our bloodstream. As discussed in Chapter 8, the most important breathing distinction is learning how to fill your lower lungs with air on a habitual basis.

OTHER IDEAS FOR 2-10 MINUTE BREAKS:

- **Meditation**: Meditation increases alpha brain waves and improves relaxation. A study performed by Dr. Bernard Glueck at the Institute for Living in Hartford, Connecticut, found that men and women practicing meditation showed an increased synchronicity between the right and left sides of the brain. One study does not a principle make, but my experience suggests that this is an excellent 5-10 minute break idea.

- **Visualization**: As mentioned in Chapter 3, I sometimes lie down on the floor somewhere in a very relaxed state with the intention of simply visualizing the software I'm developing. This is not a nap in that I remain conscious and perform various mental gymnastics. I "see" the screens in my mind and as the user makes selections, the software responds appropriately. I also use this time to mentally walk through the strategy I'm using to develop the software and to search for possible refinements. There is usually a point of diminishing returns with this process and so I usually set specific time limits to prevent loosing track of time. If you don't do these breaks ecologically, you'll tend to avoid them over time.

- **Mini-tramping**: This great ten-minute workout on a mini-trampoline is discussed in Chapter 8.

- **Juggling**: I keep a can of tennis balls in my office for this purpose. This involves coordination, timing, & dimension.

- **Drawing**: Purchase a copy of Betty Edwards' book, *Drawing on the Right Side of the Brain* and begin chipping away at this valuable skill.

- **Listening to music**: I use a portable CD player to listen to variety of music depending on which mode or mood I'm in. I have inspirational music such as *Chariots of Fire* or *Theme from Rocky*, creative music such as baroque music and Mozart, high energy music such as Bryan Adams' *Summer of 69* or Boston's *I Think I Like it*, and relaxing music such as Kenny G's *Live* album or Stephen Halpern's *Crystal Suite*.

- **Creating music**: The Miracle Keyboard, by The Software Toolworks, Inc., is a 48-key piano keyboard with full size keys, great sound (digitized recordings in ROM), and pressure-sensitive keys, all integrated with a software learning system. I recently purchased one at a local computer store for $150.

- **Nerf hoops**: This is where you hang a small plastic hoop on a door and play basketball with a soft spongy ball. These components are available at discount stores for $5-10. Nerf basketball involves dimensional thinking, which is handled by the right brain. If you've ever put in several 80-hour weeks back to back on thought-intensive work, you may understand why I've included this.

MENTAL REST

→ Your mind continues to work even while you sleep. This is one reason why it's a good idea to finish the day by writing down the six most important things you want to accomplish tomorrow. Your subconscious mind starts to work on them immediately and helps prepare you for action when you arrive at work the next day.

Sleep rests the body, but what is the best way to rest your mind and recharge your mental batteries? I learned this idea from Vernon Bowlby over ten years ago. He suggests doing an activity that completely rips you out of your mental ruts, something that you absolutely love to do. I seem to get my best mental rest from snow skiing, water skiing and boating. These things require 100% of my attention, they get me out in nature where the air is fresh and the scenery beautiful. Connecting with the beauty and magnificence of nature is a powerfully rejuvenating experience. Most importantly, they give me a chance to spend quality time with my family and friends.

It is sometimes difficult to realize just how much I need mental rest until after I've come back from a trip, so scheduling such trips on a regular basis is probably wise. The difference in my knowledge work productivity is so pronounced after one of these trips that, at least for me, violating this one rule is enough to compromise the benefits gained from every other technique suggested in this book. Nolan Bushnell, inventor of Pong and founder of Atari gets most of his most profitable new ideas when he's doing things out of his normal routine. While away from his usual surroundings in "play" mode, he believes that he allows a different part of his brain to be activated. Bushnell invented the game *Breakout* while running his fingers through the sand on a beach. He claims that his life oscillates between being a morning person and an evening person. Evening mode promotes creativity while morning mode is more conducive to getting things done.[9]

If you have ever studied weight lifting principles, you know that our best understanding to date is that you should use a one day on, one day off cycle. During the exertion, muscles are strained and to some degree torn. During the day off they repair themselves and build themselves into a stronger state than before the workout. Mental rest is the same idea applied to your mind. It is the essence of what Scott Peck, in The Road Less Traveled, calls "balancing" or disciplining discipline.

PERCEIVING TIME IN A NON-LINEAR FASHION

One way I know if an activity is giving me effective mental rest is by how I perceive time passage during the trip. If an activity is restful, time seems to slow down. Four hours cruising on the boat often feels like two whole days. Time isn't dragging along; it just feels like we've packed two days of life into those four hours. Not that we rush around on these trips. In fact, it's just the opposite. Activities are scheduled very loosely and we just "go with the flow". If you doubt the possibility of perceiving time in such a nonlinear fashion, consider the words of Paul Harvey when he asked, "How long is a minute?" After a brief pause he replied, "I guess that depends which side of the bathroom door you're on."

USING ANCHORS

You can leverage your mental rest activity by selecting a single tape of favorite music that seems in harmony with the mood of your vacation. By listening to this music periodically

---

[9] Adapted from Roger von Oech's book, *A Kick in the Seat of the Pants.*

throughout the vacation, it will "anchor" the experience. Whenever you hear songs from this tape in the future, it will tend to remind you of the state of mental rest you achieved on the vacation. (Perhaps now my friends and family will understand why I tend to play the same tape over and over on any given trip.)

A formula for burnout in knowledge work is: focus, focus, focus. By oscillating—focus, rest, focus, rest—we increase our ability to focus effectively. You might find it helpful to plan such oscillations on a daily, weekly, and project basis.

CONCLUSION

Conscious ⟵⟶ Subconscious

Individual Thought ⟵⟶ Dialogue

Left-Brain Mode ⟵⟶ **Right-Brain Mode**

Detailed Thought ⟵⟶ High Level Thought

This chapter addressed the third major strategy for using complementary opposite modes of thinking to achieve mental leverage. Hemispheric specialization is a fact, and oscillating between right and left-brain thinking is a useful way to apply this distinction. However, the principle of mental oscillation extends beyond the left/right metaphor. While the above diagram summarizes the four main types of oscillation I've chosen to emphasize in chapters 2-6, you will find traces of this principle in the remaining chapters as well.

Developing the mental flexibility to employ complementary opposite styles of thinking requires discipline. It often requires us to suspend previous training, habits and mental structures. A key strategy for maintaining ecology during such dismantling is to set specific time limits for activities involving new modes of thinking.

As discussed in this chapter, mindmaps help shift our thinking to "meta" or structural levels; this is a right brain mental process that helps get creative juices flowing. The next chapter shows how such structural thinking can be applied towards optimizing other mental processes frequently performed by knowledge workers.

EXERCISE

1) Pick the topic in this book that you would most like to learn.

2) Find someone to teach it to. This could be one or two people who you think could benefit. Or, you may want to give a five minute speech on the subject. A third alternative is to write a one or two page article for a newsletter.

3) Take out a blank sheet of unlined white paper. Turn the sheet sideways and, in the middle, either draw a small picture, symbol or a few keywords that represent the essence of the topic.

4) (Optional step) Set a timer for 2-5 minutes. A kitchen oven timer works well because the bell interrupts your pattern when it goes off. At the office, you can use the stopwatch feature of a digital watch or just write the ending time in the upper right corner of the page as a reminder. During this time, act as if you have mastered Aldous Huxley's "Profound Relaxation" technique: Relax yourself as deeply as possible and then focus on a single thought. Ask your subconscious mind to make available to you all possible knowledge on the topic you are going to brainstorm. Ask that it flow through your hand and on to the page abundantly. Stop when the timer goes off.

5) Set a timer for five minutes. This time, write as many ideas as you can think of on the subject. Use symbols, personal shorthand, keywords, any other technique you can think of to get the ideas on the page as quickly as possible.

6) Take a five minute break.

7) Scan this book for additional ideas on the subject, adding them to the idea collection sheet where you think it appropriate.

8) Take out a second sheet of paper and organize the ideas into a mindmap according to the structure of the information. This is the content of your presentation.

9) Decide on the order in which the content will be presented using one of the techniques described in this chapter.

10) Practice the delivery a couple of times and then give the presentation. Just do it, and trust that whatever resources you need to pull this off will come to you. Developing faith in this process is a "meta-lesson" of far-reaching potential.

CHAPTER 6

GOING META

"I think it is an extremely valuable thing, to train our mind to stand apart and examine its own program."
— *Stephen Covey*

"In a time of rapid change, it is the learners who inherit the future. The learned find themselves equipped to live in a world that no longer exists."
— *Eric Hoffer*

"People who learn things the fastest will do much better than those who learn things the best."
— *Paul Zane Pilzer*

"Meta" means above, so I use the phrase "going meta" to describe the process of rising above. There are two main ways of applying this distinction to knowledge work:

- Traversing the structure of information, facilitated by tools such as mindmaps.
- Traversing the structure of your thoughts in order to optimize key mental processes.

The emphasis in this chapter is on training your mind to "stand apart and examine its own program". Specifically, this chapter is about fine tuning the mental software you use to learn and interact with information.

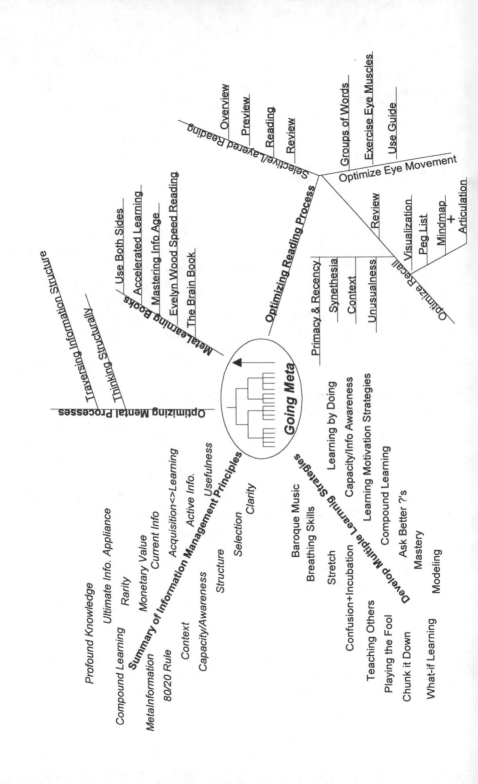

Going Meta

Optimizing Reading Process

Selective/Layered Reading
- Overview
- Preview
- Reading
- Review

Optimize Eye Movement
- Groups of Words
- Exercise Eye Muscles
- Use Guide

Optimize Recall
- Visualization
- Peg List
- Mindmap + Articulation
- Review
- Primacy & Recency
- Synesthesia
- Context
- Unusualness

Optimizing Mental Processes
- Traversing Information Structure
- Thinking Structurally

Metal Learning Books
- Use Both Sides
- Accelerated Learning
- Mastering Info Age
- Evelyn Wood Speed Reading
- The Brain Book

Summary of Information Management Principles
- Profound Knowledge
- Ultimate Info. Appliance
- Compound Learning
- Rarity
- Monetary Value
- MetaInformation
- Current Info
- 80/20 Rule
- Acquisition<>Learning
- Context
- Active Info.
- Capacity/Awareness
- Usefulness
- Structure
- Selection
- Clarity

Develop Multiple Learning Strategies
- Baroque Music
- Learning by Doing
- Breathing Skills
- Capacity/Info Awareness
- Stretch
- Learning Motivation Strategies
- Confusion+Incubation
- Compound Learning
- Teaching Others
- Ask Better ?'s
- Playing the Fool
- Mastery
- Chunk it Down
- Modeling
- What-if Learning

➜   If you find yourself doing something repeatedly, it may be worthwhile to periodically examine the process used to carry it out. I once read a study that calculated the number of hours the average person spends tying their shoes over the course of their lifetime. The amount of time was so huge that I became determined to figure out how to reduce this number. I explored ways of tying my shoes faster, and eventually started wearing shoes that just slip on and off, so I don't have to tie my shoes at all. In addition to optimizing a mental process, sometimes there are ways of organizing yourself so that certain activities are no longer necessary.

The amount of information with which knowledge workers must interact has increased significantly throughout my career, a trend likely to continue. This chapter presents a number of distinctions you can use to optimize processes performed frequently while interacting with information in ways such as reading, remembering and learning.

These ideas were inspired by Tony Buzan's book, *Use Both Sides of Your Brain*. Buzan taught me that it is one thing to read a book about a specific topic such as science or math, and quite another to read a book that improves the way I read every book from that point forward. Buzan's ideas took me from reading 50 books every couple years, to extracting useful information from 50 books every couple months. This increase in my information metabolism led me to four other metalearning books:

- *Accelerated Learning*, by Colin Rose
- *Mastering the Information Age*, by Michael J. McCarthy
- *Remember Everything You Read: The 7 Day Evelyn Wood Speed Reading Program,* by Stanley D. Frank
- *The Brain Book*, by Peter Russell

Many of the ideas presented in these books are directed at students. This chapter explains just a few of their ideas as I've been able to apply them at work. My goal with this chapter is to sell you on the potential value of such metalearning, and thus encourage you to read, at a minimum, the above books by Rose and McCarthy.

→ Before diving into this chapter, I want to emphasize that the notion of "going meta" can be applied to more than just mental process optimization. For example, you may want to have an occasional "metadiscussion". This is a discussion about the structure or format of the conversation you are having with someone. It goes something like this:

> "I'd just like to take a moment to make sure that there isn't anything about the way I'm communicating with you that is abrasive. I know my attempts to do things creatively sometimes cut across established boundaries, and I want to make sure that you feel comfortable openly expressing any concerns you have about my methods."

Another example of how individuals can optimize non-mental processes is typing. Why does it make sense that some of the fastest typists I've ever seen are programmers for Microsoft? Because the faster they can type, the faster they can program, all other things being equal. By optimizing a process repeatedly performed when programming, they've eliminated a potential performance bottleneck.

The point is to keep your eyes peeled for any activity that you repeatedly perform (or need to perform). It may be worth your while to invest some thought and/or practice into optimizing such activities. And by considering the context in which that process is performed, you may even discover ways of achieving the same benefit without having to tie your shoes at all.

OPTIMIZING THE READING PROCESS

One of my favorite scenes from the TV sitcom "Taxi" was when Alex was rapidly flipping through the pages of a book in traditional speed reading style. Elaine walks up and says, "Alex, so you're taking that speed reading course—what are you reading?" Alex responds, "I haven't the foggiest idea."

→   I took a speed reading class in high school, and was left with pretty much the same impression—a belief that speed reading had no substance to it. This perception changed when I read *Using Both Sides of Your Brain* by Tony Buzan. This book increased my information metabolism by teaching me both how to tie my shoes faster and pointing out cases where I didn't need to tie them at all. Rather than learning to become a speed reader, he taught me how to become a "speed understander". In summary, he teaches how to:

- Read more selectively
- Optimize the way you use your eyes
- Optimize the process you use to remember key ideas

The following discussion elaborates on the above themes by synthesizing ideas from several related books.

READING MORE SELECTIVELY

The underlying principle is this:

> As the amount of information increases in a given area, there is an increasing need for the ability to scan that information at a high level and to be highly selective of the areas you choose to study in detail.

When I read anything, my objective is not to look at every word and picture as fast as I can. Rather, it is to identify and understand useful ideas as efficiently as possible, and then to either transfer this information to long term memory or note it for future reference.

Imagine arriving at a large lake and being told that somewhere in the water there is a buried treasure. To find that treasure, you could either put on your trunks and go for a swim, or jump in a high speed boat with radar programmed to detect the presence of anything resembling the treasure. This would allow you to do a fairly quick pass over the entire lake, noting areas that look promising, and then go back to each promising location, drop anchor, and go for a dive. You are much more likely to find the treasure because you will have eliminated huge portions of the lake very quickly.

When it comes to reading, your subconscious mind is your radar, and it is "programmed" when you invest time "self-communicating" the outcome you are trying to create.

Of course, when it comes to reading selectively, the most important thing is to make sure you are swimming in the right lake! Any time I'm presented with an information rich environment, such as a bookstore or a trade convention like COMDEX, I invest time up front getting clear on my goals, and then do some high speed scans over the entire terrain before diving into a single book or booth. It often takes discipline to finish the complete scan before stopping at an extremely promising location. Ray Dolby, inventor of Dolby noise reduction, encourages would-be inventors not to jump at the first solution because sometimes the really elegant solution is right around the corner.

I have just described a rather left-brain approach to reading. Its complementary opposite is to allocate some time looking for the unexpected. The key to this strategy is to set a specific time limit, since we tend to ignore time when operating in right-brain mode. My experience suggests that without the discipline of setting specific time limits for "right-brain" mode activities, there is a tendency to avoid them in order to maintain personal ecology.

LAYERED READING

In addition to using your subconscious mental radar, you can read books more selectively by using a layered reading approach. Here are four phases that commonly show up in layered reading strategies:

- **Overview**: Look over the entire book at the rate of 1 second per page to determine its organization, structure and tone. Try to finish the overview in 5 minutes.
- **Preview**: Should you decide to read further, preview the first chapter at the rate of 4 seconds per page. Pay

particular attention to beginnings and endings such as the introduction and conclusion, and the first sentences of paragraphs and sections. Mark key sections with Post-it tabs or a yellow marker.

- **Read**: If any part of the chapter warrants closer attention, go back and read it at whatever speed seems appropriate.
- **Review**: As discussed in the following section on memory, doing short reviews periodically after reading new ideas can significantly increase the amount of detailed information that makes it into long term memory.

There are several advantages to having seen every page of a document. It partially eliminates the intimidation of the unknown. It is also much easier to comprehend material at rapid speeds when your eyes have already seen the material twice, even if only briefly. And lastly, your right brain is a lot happier about the whole situation because it has at least some idea of the context or overall picture in which the material is being presented.

Saying that someone has one reading speed is like having a car that only goes one speed. Different material calls for different speeds. Layered reading is about being flexible in the strategy you use to extract useful ideas from written material.

Here are some additional suggestions for reading more selectively:

- Focus on key words and ignore filler words. As discussed in the previous chapter, most of the meaning in sentences is transferred by a few key words. Many times it is unnecessary to read all the "is's" and "the's".
- Skip what you already know. As you transfer more and more knowledge from an area into long term memory, the sections you can skip will become larger and thus accelerate your journey along the compound learning curve.

- Skip material that doesn't apply to you.
- Skip material that seems particularly confusing and come back to it if necessary after reading other sections. Books are linear while their subject matter is often multi-dimensional. As Hannah Arendt put it, "Nothing we use or hear or touch can be expressed in words that equal what we are given by the senses." It may be far easier to understand the material in light of information that follows. Giving your subconscious time to incubate the material might help as well.

OPTIMIZING EYE MOVEMENT

→   Obviously we use our eyes a lot when we read, so it makes sense to examine the processes involved in the interest of optimization. This section discusses three aspects of eye involvement: reading groups of words, exercising your eye muscles, and using a guide.

READING GROUPS OF WORDS

It turns out that our eyes can only take in information when they are stopped. What feels like continuous motion is actually move-stop-read-move-stop-read, etc. You can easily verify this by sitting face to face with a partner, holding one finger up, and watching their eyes as you move your finger in a circular motion or even side to side. The key is to minimize the number of stops by maximizing the number of words you see at each stop as shown in Figure 6.1.

The person who uses the first eye movement pattern is actually looking at every word, one at a time. The person who uses the second is still looking at every word, but in groups. The person who uses the third eye movement pattern "notices" only a few key words and does so by reading both horizontally and vertically at the same time.

"But the first reader is going to comprehend the material much better than the third!" you may be thinking. Possibly, is my reply. If the third reader actually uses all three eye movement patterns, using the slower patterns very selectively, then he has a better chance of investing his mental energies on the material of most relevance to him.

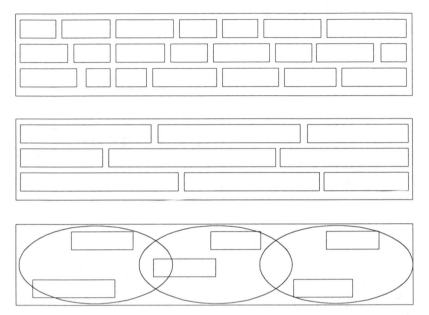

Figure 6.1. Three eye movement patterns.

"The art of becoming wise is the art of knowing what to overlook."

— William James

The third reader is much more likely to find the treasure chest in the information lake than the first reader who just wades in with no flippers. The smart reader is one who uses the third technique to scan the entire book (overview) or chapter (preview), and then comes back and uses some combination of the first two techniques to further explore the sections of most interest.

Getting to both the second and third levels requires a visual reading strategy. You must silence subvocalization and learn to "trust your eyes". This involves shifting your mental

reading   process   from   "see→say→understand"   to   just
"see→understand". One way to make this leap is to build up
your visualization muscle using the exercises suggested in
Chapter 3 and later on in this chapter.

273	_____	11454	_____	17 44 34	_____
545	_____	87879	_____	86 32 77	_____
142	_____	12342	_____	65 41 28	_____
275	_____	45411	_____	27 33 11	_____
848	_____	78989	_____	66 32 97	_____
109	_____	21314	_____	32 45 81	_____
2763	_____	56548	_____	44 18 72	_____
5478	_____	09711	_____	31 73 90	_____
4452	_____	33442	_____	27 11 88	_____
1127	_____	83219	_____	72 61 49	_____
9956	_____	76675	_____	16 64 34	_____
3313	_____	33228	_____	26 89 55	_____

Figure 6.2. Grouping Exercise.

The exercise shown in Figure 6.2 was adapted from material
in *Speed Reading* by Tony Buzan. It will help you train your
eyes to take in words in larger gulps. Begin by coverting the
numbers with a sheet of paper. Then uncover one at a time
for a fraction of a second. From memory, write the number
you saw to the right. The idea is to increase the amount of
information taken in with each glance. To make it more
challenging, try uncovering two numbers at once.

→ Our   brains   are   capable   of   receiving   and   processing
information hundreds of times faster than we ordinarily read.
Slow   reading   keeps   the   brain   challenged.   Reading   faster
forces the brain to pay attention and keeps it interested.

Before pitching a game in little league, I used to go into my
friend's backyard and throw an extremely heavy softball a
few times (after some warm-up of course). When the time

came to pitch the normal size baseball, it felt so small and light that I was able to throw it much faster than most pitchers my age. I pitched the last 5 games of the season without giving up a single hit. Granted, there were many other factors, but I have no doubt that my "softball" ritual played a part. You can use this same technique to improve your reading speed. Periodically read "as if" you could read 3-5 times your best speed. Stay relaxed, breathing fully and rhythmically while you do this.

Several of these ideas are based on the "visual-vertical" strategy taught in the Evelyn Wood program. For the upcoming class schedules, call (800) 447-7323. This strategy is also covered by Stanley Frank in his book, *Remember Everything You Read, The Evelyn Wood 7 Day Speed Reading and Learning Program*.

EXERCISING EYE MUSCLES

➜ In Richard Hittleman's Yoga teachings, he recommends the following exercise for strengthening your eye muscles:

1) Close your eyes for a moment, then open them.
2) Without moving your head, look up as high as you can go without straining.
3) That's 12 o'clock. Now move your eyes around the numbers of the clock, pausing briefly at each number on the clock.
4) Go around twice counter-clockwise and twice clockwise, pausing for a moment after each circle.

USING A GUIDE

➜ Question: How do you know when someone is "speed reading?" Answer: They're running their fingers up and down each page. Evelyn Wood discovered the idea of using a guide to improve reading speed and comprehension. After studying the fastest readers she could find, one day she dropped a book in the dirt. She picked up the book and brushed off each page only to discover that she had basically read the book. Using a guide does four things: it helps prevent the mind from wandering, it helps keep your eyes focused on the right part of the page, it limits the number of fixations per page which encourages bigger "gulps" of information, and, by deliberately speeding up your guide, it will help your eyes move faster. When reading material on a computer screen, you can use the mouse pointer as your guide instead of your fingers.

This "S" pattern works well for the preview and reading phases, but I use a different method for doing high speed overviews in an effort to minimize hand movement and maximize speed. I hold the left page 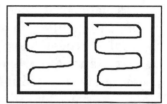 with the left hand and the right page with the right hand. The left hand starts at the top of the left page. As the left hand moves down the left page, the right hand moves to the top of the right page and prepares to turn it. When the left hand reaches the bottom of the left page, I begin moving it back up the page as my gaze moves to the top of the right page. My right hand begins moving down the right page with only my thumb on the side of the page that I'm reading. In effect I'm scanning the right page as I turn it. When my right thumb reaches the bottom of the right page, I finish turning the page and begin moving my right hand up into position to scan and turn the next page.

In summary then, the key variables that determine how fast you read are:

- How long you stop at each place.
- How many words or how much area on the page you take in at each stop.
- How long it takes you to move your eyes to the next stopping point.
- The degree to which you minimize backskipping.
- The extent to which you mentally bypass your internal dialogue system as you read.

- Your state of mind and body at the time you are reading. This includes factors such as alpha brain wave activity, energy level, breathing technique, level of interest in the material, clarity about why you are reading the material, and beliefs regarding the potential benefits.
- The percentage of the material you already know, which to some extent depends upon how much you remember material you've read in the past.

OPTIMIZING THE PROCESS OF REMEMBERING

The more information about a topic you have transferred into long term memory such that it can be recalled easily on demand, the faster you can take in new material on that subject. Long term memory is where your Social Security number is stored. The key question becomes "What is the most efficient method of transferring information from short term into long term memory?" There are several memory tricks available, but the four that have given me the most benefit are:

- Using short periodic review sessions
- Developing my mental "visualization" muscle
- Drawing mindmaps
- Articulation

The following sections explore these themes in more detail.

USING SHORT PERIODIC REVIEW SESSIONS

→ Performing 2-3 minute reviews of material 10 minutes, 24 hours, one week and one month after initial learning helps transfer more of the ideas into long term memory in a way that they can be recalled quickly. This strategy comes from *Using Both Sides of Your Brain* by Tony Buzan. While the idea is useful, trying to follow it exactly creates something of a scheduling nightmare. I am learning so many things from so many sources, that it is virtually impossible to overlap review sessions for all ideas into my schedule.

In practice, the 10 minute review session is the easiest to perform. I just set the material down for a few minutes and do something else. I then come back and review the ideas for a couple of minutes before completely moving on to the next topic. The 24-hour review usually ends up being some time the next day, if I get a chance to review it at all. I like to read in the evening before going to bed, so I just scan the highlighted material from the previous night before moving on to the next section.

I get hit with new ideas via e-mail and other sources throughout the day. Scheduling review sessions for this material is more difficult. If the e-mail is important, I just leave it open after reading it the first time, and then close the window the next day after a quick review.

Regarding the one-week and one-month review sessions, well, if I don't end up using the information within that time period, then it probably wasn't worth a third or fourth review anyway. For material in books, I occasionally do "library reviews", where I spend two hours rapidly flipping through as many books in my library as possible within the time limit. This is where the yellow highlighted material and Post-it tabs really pay off.

Audiotapes lend themselves well to the review process. Because they can be listened to in the car, it is much easier to listen to a tape several times than it is to read a book several times. The disadvantage is that we don't as yet have a way to "yellow highlight" an audiotape for selective review.

DEVELOPING YOUR VISUALIZATION MUSCLE

➜   Every book and tape program I've found on improving memory has you perform exercises to develop your ability to visualize and manipulate pictures in your mind's eye. They suggest several memory tools based on this skill, such as peg lists and picture stories, which I've found difficult to apply in the fast paced information blitz of day to day work. However, the exercises did mobilize latent memory capacities that seem to spill over into several aspects of my work. By having done the exercises, and by applying them in certain situations, I seem to be doing something in my mind that has improved my ability to remember things in all situations. The following mini-version of the peg list exercise will give you an idea of the principles involved.

Peg lists show up in almost all memory training books. This technique involves committing a series of number-picture associations to long term memory, and then using them whenever you need to remember lists of things. For example, here is a list of number-picture associations for the numbers one through five:

1) Space Needle, since it looks like the number one
2) Door, since it has two positions, either opened or closed
3) Stool, since it has three legs
4) Horse, since it has four legs
5) Star, since it has five points

The first step is to memorize this list so completely that when anyone mentions any number, you immediately can think of the picture, and vice-versa. You should be able to walk the list forwards and backwards. This is an excellent chance to try the periodic review strategy discussed in the last section. Try writing them out several times, or calling a friend and describe this weird memory exercise which involves a list of five items, "a Space Needle, a door, etc."

Once this peg list has been transferred to long term memory, you are ready to use it to remember a list of items. For example, let's say you needed to remember to perform the following five tasks tomorrow and didn't have a pencil to write them in your schedule:

1) Call Joe
2) Meet with Sue Carpenter
3) E-mail Acorn project team
4) Read new "Snowball" strategy report

5) Write bubble sort routine

In your mind you could associate the above tasks to your peg list items as follows:

- Imagine a G.I. Joe army figure climbing the outside of the Space Needle with a giant telephone in one hand while shouting "Call Me" in Pig Latin.
- Imagine a carpenter working on your office door telling you as you walk in that you are likely to get sued if it doesn't get fixed.
- Imagine your team members standing on a bunch of stools under an oak tree picking acorns and throwing them into a mail bag.
- Imagine riding a horse reading the report as the horse balances on a snowball plowing down a hill over your competitors.
- Imagine a pen full of star shaped bubbles with numbers on them that float up in sorted order.

The next day when you get to work, you ask, "What was the first thing on my list?" This triggers the memory of the Space Needle, which triggers the memory of G.I. Joe climbing it shouting "allCay eMay" and so forth. While this probably seems ridiculous, it is a great exercise for strengthening your visualization muscle.

There are some drawbacks to using peg lists in day to day work. In addition to taking a fair amount of time to dream up word pictures for each item I want to remember, there is the issue of figuring out how to manage all the different lists. You almost need a peg list to remember your peg lists. Additionally, it is more difficult to apply this technique to a list of concepts than a list of objects.

Another reason I don't fill my mind with ludicrous imagery on a habitual basis is that thoughts are things. Any time you think a thought, you increase the probability that it will come into existence. Lastly, once you develop the skill of being able to create, remember and manipulate visual images deftly in your mind, you must discipline your use of this skill. You must be careful to limit your mind to positive imagery or at least use negative imagery with extreme caution.

MINDMAPS AND ACTIVE READING

The process of creating the mindmap promotes active reading and encourages you to think about the structure of the information being read. When completed, mindmaps facilitate quick reviews.

Oftentimes the most valuable aspect of drawing a mindmap is the impact the process has on your understanding and memory of the material. It doesn't matter so much what it looks like on paper as much as what went on in your head while you were drawing it. There are often useful ideas contained in the way the ideas relate to each other, which are not apparent when the ideas are viewed sequentially. The more information you try to put on the page, the harder it becomes to locate any particular idea. I feel that they are best used as a gestalt tool.

Creating a bunch of mindmaps poses a problem: what do you do with mindmaps when you're done? At work I store them in the related project folder, at home they go in my journal or in the book on which they are based.

USE VISUALIZATION PLUS ARTICULATION

→   Socrates encouraged students to articulate, thereby drawing forth existing knowledge and sharpening their perception of new material. Articulation also facilitates and deepens your memory of new material. A simple use of this distinction is to discuss useful ideas with a friend during the return trip from a seminar. Another application combines the use of mindmaps, visualization and review discussed earlier. If you sketch a mindmap while reading or hearing new material, then during your 2-3 minute review sessions, you can take a mental snapshot of the mindmap, close your eyes, and begin articulating the content of that mindmap as if you were teaching a class.

SUMMARY OF OTHER MEMORY DISTINCTIONS

While the above four topics offer the most leverage for improving your memory, there are a few other distinctions that play a role:

- **Primacy and Recency**: We tend to remember the first and last ideas more than the ones in between. This means that many short sessions are better than a single long one, because you will have more firsts and lasts.
- **Synesthesia**: The more sensory experience you incorporate into your memories, the more likely you are to remember them. As Colin Rose describes in his book, *Accelerated Learning*, the Russian psychologist, Professor Luria, spent 30 years studying a man named Shereshevskii (referred to as S.), who consistently exhibited perfect recall over long periods (several years). In addition to having amazing visualization skills, he was also adept in synesthesia, which is the ability to express a memory generated in one sense in terms of another. For example, S described a tone with a pitch of 2,000 cycles per second as looking something like fireworks with a pink-red hue. S continued, "The strip of color feels rough and unpleasant, and it has an ugly taste—rather like that of a briny pickle."
- **Context:** Ideas are easier to remember when they can be associated to a specific context.
- **Unusualness:** Things remembered more easily if they stand out from the ordinary in our minds, which is why Kevin Trudeau's Megamemory course emphasizes the use of outrageous and ludicrous multisensory imagery.

DEVELOP MULTIPLE LEARNING STRATEGIES

➔   Just as it is useful to develop multiple reading strategies which can be applied flexibly, it is also worthwhile to have multiple learning strategies. Peter Senge offers three excellent distinctions about learning:

- All learning occurs over time.
- All learning involves a continual movement between a world of thought and a world of action. No action, no learning.
- Knowledge is distributed throughout the body.

He points out that the Chinese symbol for learning consists of two symbols, one meaning "study" and the other "practice constantly". The Chinese cannot think the thought "learning" without simultaneously thinking the thought "practice constantly". Too often in our culture the "practice constantly" part is left out to the point where people think they "know" something just because they read about it.

There are as many strategies for learning as there are topics to learn about. Your effectiveness as a learner is impacted by the breadth and depth of your repertoire of learning strategies, and your ability to switch between them as the learning situation demands. Maslow's statement about all of your problems looking like nails if your only tool is a hammer also applies here. As you expand your awareness of these techniques, you are likely to expand the extent to which you notice opportunities to use them. The following material describes a sampling of the more effective strategies I've come across. Sometimes the best strategy is a combination of all of them.

I trust that you will use excellent judgment in selecting learning strategies appropriate for each situation.

I just noticed that the baby pine tree I've been raising has outgrown its pot. Planting this tree in soil without the restrictions of a pot will allow its root structure to expand more freely, and the tree above ground will soon grow to reflect this new fundamental flexibility. Similarly, being limited in the strategies you use to learn can limit your personal growth. Let's see if we can knock down a few walls.

"The only kind of understanding that I'm interested in is the kind that allows you to do something."

— Richard Bandler

LEARNING BY DOING

The solutions approach is my overall strategy for learning. "Do the thing and you will have the power," wrote Emerson. This strategy seems to work best when the "thing" is solving somebody elses real-world problem.

> *"By any definition, and in any disguise, problem solving is a heuristic process—a process of trial and error."*
>
> *—— Ken Orr*

You can read about something until you are blue in the face, but until you are presented with an opportunity to actually apply the material, your "learning" has not even gotten off the ground. It is for this reason that I agree with John Dewey when he says, "Cease conceiving of education as mere preparation for later life, and make of it the full meaning of the present life...An activity which does not have worth enough to be carried out for its own sake cannot be very effective as a preparation for something else." Dewey's motto was "learning by doing". It is my sincere hope that high schools will encourage students to begin taking on projects in their chosen field while still in school. The idea is to get them involved in project teams and an overall process closely aligned with the work they will do when they graduate. This experience would give them a context in which they can understand how the material learned in school is useful.

> *"The great aim of education is not knowledge but action."*
>
> *—— Herbert Spencer*

CAPACITY/INFORMATION AWARENESS THEORY

I once read that reading is 90% mental and only 10% eye movement. This makes sense when you consider that we are not just piling a bunch of words into our brains when we read. Words are symbols which are translated into ideas and organized into a useful context. Aldous Huxley touched on this notion when he wrote, "Knowledge is a function of being. When there is a change in the being of the knower, there is a corresponding change in the nature and amount of knowledge."

At the end of Chapter 1, I posed the question: "What can a person do to increase the rate at which they are ready for new learning?" In Chapter 2, I suggested taking on a series of projects of increasing complexity that demands new learning.

I believe that our awareness of information expands according to our capacity to use it. Doing something to increase your information handling capacity will tend to expand the amount of information you are aware of. Buying a new bookshelf, filing cabinet, a larger hard disk, or implementing a new system for managing the flow ideas in your life, can all have this effect. The survival instinct built into our subconscious mind tends to block information from our awareness to the extent that making practical use of that information is beyond our ability.

If you buy a bigger hard disk, you can load more software and do more things with your personal computer. If you buy a new bookcase, you can organize your books better and thus reference them more effectively when needed. If you purchase a new time management system where you can log new ideas that pop into your head and review them periodically, you will be more likely to benefit from those ideas, and this will encourage more of them to "arrive". The most useful part of my time management system is the address book I carry around. This has dramatically extended my capacity to interact with my network of contacts, who have in their heads the most useful information I can access.

My suggestion is that by enhancing your capacity to organize information usefully, you expand the scope of information you can be aware of and still maintain ecology. This takes us back to the solutions approach discussed in

Chapter 2. Projects give us problems to solve and provide a framework for making use of vast quantities of information.

EFFECTIVE LEARNING MOTIVATION STRATEGIES

Neuro Linguistic Programming (NLP) is a vast and rich set of distinctions for thinking at "meta" levels. One aspect of NLP involves information about the structure of our thoughts—distinctions that can be used to alter the degree to which you are motivated to do something.

As described in Chapter 3, NLP breaks down subjective experience into submodalities. An example of a motivation strategy might be: you feel a certain sensation, hear a certain voice and then see a certain picture. In his book, *Using Your Brain,* Richard Bandler states that people often motivate themselves by making mental pictures of themselves doing pleasant things. They are usually so attracted to these pictures that they just start doing them. Bandler points out that this process doesn't work for motivating yourself to complete tasks you don't like to do, like taxes. Making pictures of doing taxes can be repelling.

Bandler also comes across a lot of people who motivate themselves by thinking about how bad they will feel if they don't do something, and then move away from that bad feeling. Others use pleasant feelings to move toward what they do want to have happen, and give themselves reinforcement along the way. They do this by thinking about how great it feels to have each piece done. Bandler believes the key to getting started on a task is to access that feeling of being done ahead of time.

You have to be careful when upgrading your motivation strategies. Bandler points out that while some people are lousy decision-makers, they aren't very motivated so they don't get into much trouble. Before he teaches someone a powerful new motivation strategy, Bandler makes sure they have an effective strategy for making decisions. This helps ensure that people are motivated to do things that are personally ecological for them. More on this in Chapter 9.

Another case in *Using Your Brain* describes how a successful businessman in Oregon uses NLP to enhance his ability to complete a task:

1) Make a slide - a single picture of the task to be done.
2) Expand the slide to make it panoramic - so it fills his entire field of vision in his mind's eye.
3) Step inside the picture and convert it to a movie.
4) Any time he has trouble seeing where the movie is going, he steps back slightly (i.e., pulls himself out of the movie). As soon as the movie starts up again, he steps back inside.

This man does not distinguish between understanding something and being able to do it. I ran into a few difficulties when apply this strategy myself. First of all, knowledge work has a conceptual element that is not easily represented with a picture. Secondly, I needed to distinguish between "how" thinking, which is extremely detailed, and "what" thinking (i.e., outcome clarification). And finally, my projects often last several weeks or months, and while I'm getting faster at "playing mental movies", I'm not yet able to condense a few hundred hours of movies into an hour or two of thinking. What I ended up doing is creating a series of pictures that represented successful milestones along the way. For each milestone, I created a series of pictures or scenes that would lead to that milestone—things that needed to be done consistently to achieve the milestone. With these at hand, I could then apply the above strategy to each milestone. At a higher level, I could play a series of scenes that just represented the actual achievement of each milestone.

COMPOUND LEARNING

If learning seems difficult at first, keep in mind that it will become easier to learn as you begin to climb the compound learning curve. This involves maximizing the amount of related information you transfer to long-term memory so that it can be easily recalled at a conscious level. The memory process is based on linking and association. The fewer items transfered to long term memory, the less the likelihood that new items will be registered and connected.

If you use the memory enhancing strategies discussed earlier to transfer new ideas into long term memory, knowledge will begin to compound as interest does in a savings account. With each new learning experience, the percentage of material that is "new" will 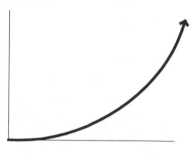 diminish, which will increase the rate at which you can assimilate the new material.

Another reason learning compounds is that some ideas will actually increase your capacity for new information. For example, if you learn one idea that increases your energy level by 5% and you actually apply the idea, the benefits from this distinction compound daily. If you develop the discipline necessary to use that extra 5% in the pursuit of additional knowledge, it could increase the rate at which you discover additional distinctions. The benefits from these distinctions begin to pile up and can potentially impact your effectiveness by several hundred percent. One percent improvement every day adds up to much more than 365%.

The flip side of the learning equation is that the more you open your mind up to the vastness of potential research material, the more you realize how important it is to specialize in one particular area that suits your particular strengths and talents. You begin to channel an increasing percentage of your research time in refining your distinctions in this specialty area. With each seminar you attend on the topic, the amount of new material presented begins to shrink. At some point, you begin to know more about the topic than most of the attendees and sometimes even the seminar leaders. After maintaining this focus and daily habit of refinement to the point where your knowledge/skill momentum reaches critical mass, you become the one creating the new breakthrough material in your field. You have become a "Master".

MASTERY

An individual high on the compound learning curve in a specific area can be a great source of learning. These individuals have maintained prolonged focus and determination to acquire daily distinctions in a specific area to the point where they are not just twice as knowledgeable as the average person in their field, but several times more knowledgeable.

For example, in the computer field, the great programmers are not just 2 or 3 times better than most, but dozens or even hundreds of times more effective.

You may recall the story of the power plant that shut down to the point where none of the company workers could get it running again. They ended up calling in a retired engineer who quickly analyzed the situation, walked over to a specific area and tapped on a pipe. The plant immediately came to life. When the company received his bill it was for $1,000.02, broken down as follows: $.02 for tapping the pipe, and $1,000 for knowing where to tap.

> *"Champions start out to be the best at what they do and then work every day towards the achievement of this goal. To be #1."*
>
> *— Mark McCormack*

Masters know exactly "where to tap" in their particular areas of specialization. I've learned a great deal from several "masters" of mental effectiveness, and you will see references to their work throughout this book. When masters write or speak, it is clear that for every word spoken, they know from 10 to 1,000 times more material on the subject than they are sharing. They have the luxury of choosing the precise content they feel perfectly matches the spirit of the moment.

To become a master in your field, consider Earl Nightingale's advice in his audiotape series *The New Lead the Field*. He suggested that by investing one hour a day doing research in your specialty area, you'll eventually leave the competition in the dust.

When reading in a new field of study, it is useful to continue doing high level scans of all related material until you feel fairly certain that you have identified the current masters. They are often the ones that are referred to the most by others. In other cases, you will recognize them by the quality of the ideas they present and the work they produce.

MODELING

It seems easier to achieve a goal if I've seen someone else do it, or if I know someone who has done it. For one thing, this changes my beliefs about what is possible. Secondly, it gives me the opportunity to observe their actions and strategies, and to listen to how they think about what they have done. People who accomplish extraordinary things act and think very differently from those who do not. In many cases, the written word does not measure up to the information our senses provide us when an act is observed in person or on video. You must hear the whole song, not just an individual note. So it is with useful ideas. Seeing them in action, within the context in which they are applied, can be more valuable than the idea itself.

The potential value of studying highly successful people has been clearly demonstrated: Dr. Georgi Lozanov studied the fastest learners and memorizers; Bandler and Grinder studied effective change agents; Anthony Robbins studied the world's most effective sales people; Evelyn Wood studied the fastest readers.

Bandler and Grinder have refined this process of observation into a technique they call modeling. Anthony Robbins used these techniques to obtain his blackbelt in tae kwon do in just eight months by modeling Grand Master Jhoon Rhee. Robbins had the benefit of being a business partner of John Grinder for several months. The best book I've found on NLP modeling techniques is *Skills for the Future*[10] by Robert Dilts. In his book, Dilts applies these skills toward modeling the creative thinking processes of Walt Disney.

In addition, an excellent article on this topic by Carmine Baffa, Ph.D. can be found at the following NLP web page:

html://www.actwin.com:80/NLP/random/genius.htm[11]

What people do has a structure. Modeling is about discovering the structure of an effective behavior pattern. The emphasis is on *what* a person does, not *why*. To model someone, ask "What does this person do inside her head that I can learn to do?" While a modeler can't instantly have the fine tuning that results from years of experience, you can quickly obtain some highly useful information about the structure of what she does.

Modeling is a substantial topic based on the notion that most of what a person does inside their head has some outward manifestation. Modeling effectiveness is largely achieved by developing the sensory acuity to notice these behavior signals and understanding what internal representations must have triggered them. A major source of such information is eye movement patterns, which are amazingly consistent throughout the human race.

A second major component of an effective modeling strategy is rapport skills. Obviously a person who likes you is more likely to share their secrets. However, modeling rapport is a bit more refined. Our bodies act much like tuning

---

[10] Available from Meta Publications by calling (408) 464-0254.

[11] If this page gets moved, refer to the *Brain Dancing Online* website discussed in Appendix B for an updated pointer.

mechanisms. If you use your physiology in the exact same way as another person, they will tend to feel more comfortable around you (i.e., a person with a nasal voice feels more comfortable around other people with nasal voices). Additionally, mirroring someone's physiology sends similar messages to your brain, thereby giving you access to what they are thinking. Anthony Robbins' seminars give you a chance to experience this phenomenon first hand.

On of the most powerful ways of doing this is to mirror breathing patterns. Peripheral vision is very effective at detecting movement, and can be used to avoid staring at a persons' chest during a conversation. Try looking at a computer monitor with your peripheral vision and notice if the screen appears to be flickering.

USING MODELING TO IMPROVE READING SPEED

If you ever catch yourself reading extremely rapidly with high comprehension, take a moment to examine the "structure" of that experience. If you can determine the precise physical, mental and environmental conditions that support this level of performance, then you may be able to reproduce them more consistently. Ask yourself questions such as:

Physiology:

- How is my energy level? What factors contributed to it being the way it is?
- Am I relaxed, or carrying tension in certain parts of my body?
- How am I breathing?
- How am I sitting? Am I leaning slightly forward? What position are my shoulders in? How am I holding the book?
- Am I tapping my foot or moving my hands across the page in a certain way?

Internal Representations (Mental Focus):

- What am I telling myself will be the benefits from being able to extract information rapidly?
- What beliefs do I have about the quality of the material and what contributed to those beliefs?
- Is there time pressure and where did it come from?
- Am I trying to "read" the material or just extract information relative to the task at hand?

Environment:

- How is the lighting? Does the room have good air circulation? Is the temperature warm or cold?

If you know someone who consistently reads fast, you may also want to apply the above questions to them.

WHAT-IF LEARNING

As you will read in the next chapter, "what-if" learning is an important strategy for learning software faster. By investing time up front to identify actions to avoid, and by minimizing the amount of time it takes to do a single experiment, you position yourself to perform a series of quick experiments that will lead you incrementally to the solution. The opposite of this strategy is to sit and wonder what would happen if you did something.

> *"Our aim, must be to make our successive mistakes as quickly as possible."*
>
> *— Karl Popper*

CHUNK IT DOWN

How do you eat an elephant? One bite at a time. Anytime you are overwhelmed by a task, step back to see if it can be broken into smaller tasks. Creating a one-page list of subtasks to check off is often a big step towards completion.

FOCUS ON RULES

Just as the process of learning a language can be simplified by first learning the rules of grammar, the process of learning software can often be simplified by memorizing syntax rules. This gives you less to remember when you see a complex application of those rules, in part because it can be encoded in terms of things you already know. "This is what math and science is all about," states Richard Bandler in *Using Your Brain*, " – coding the world efficiently and elegantly, so that you have fewer things to remember, leaving your brain free to do other things that are more fun and interesting."

ASK BETTER QUESTIONS

As mentioned previously, questions impact what we focus on. Every learning situation presents a combination of two types of information: interesting and useful. The following question will help keep you focused on useful ideas: "What am going to do differently as a result of learning this?" Here are a couple more: "If I focused all of my efforts on fully implementing just one idea learned today, what one distinction out of all this material would have the greatest long term impact on my life?" One more: "What has to happen for me to apply what I just learned (i.e., acquire emotional resources, partners, additional knowledge, etc.)?"

PLAYING THE FOOL

Ralph Waldo Emerson writes in *Compensation,* "A great man is always willing to be little." Sitting on the cushion of advantages can sometimes lull us to sleep. When someone or something puts us on our wits by making us aware of a weakness in our character, we have a chance to learn something. Obviously this strategy must be applied selectively. Wisdom is knowing when it is appropriate to question deep attitudinal assumptions that may be compromising our effectiveness. I must confess spending hours trying to fully understand the wisdom in the following statement by Burke: "No man ever had a point of pride that did not prove injurous to him."

TEACH OTHERS

"He is base,—and that is the one base thing in the universe,——to receive favors and render none," writes Emerson. Creating an opportunity to "render favors", such as teaching others who can benefit from the information in some way, is one means of increasing your capacity to "receive favors".

RAPID CONFUSION + INCUBATION

Confusion is an indication that you are on your way to understanding. Can you think of a topic that once confused the heck out of you, but which you now understand completely and apply regularly? When Peter Senge stated that "all learning occurs over time," I believe he was referring to the process of incubation. When exposed to new ideas, our subconsciousness mind (software) begins to "chew" on the information even after we walk away from it. New ideas encourage new dendrites to form in our brain (hardware). The result is that the next time we get back to the material, it seems less confusing, until gradually it becomes understood and applied.

According to Tony Buzan, creating and using new mental pathways promotes more efficient thinking. He believes that the boundaries of human intelligence are directly related to our ability to create and use new mental patterns and connections.

This distinction encourages me to broaden my range of activities, and, when learning a new topic, to accelerate my confusion rate. I begin by confusing myself as quickly as possible with as much of the material as I can. This puts time on my side via the principle of incubation. Of course there are times when I wished I'd never learned this—times where the feeling of overwhelm is a bit overwhelming. At least so far, it appears worthwhile to weather the storm.

STRETCH YOUR COMFORT ZONE

We must constantly guard ourselves against the feeling that we have learned something just because we "know" about it. You may have looked at 1,000 mindmaps and memorized every rule regarding their formation, but you haven't learned how to mindmap until you begin to draw them. Many forms of learning are passive, yet the highest leverage comes from active learning. Will Durant's enjoinder, "Not to think unless we have to" also translates into, "Not to learn unless we have to," so give yourself a reason to learn something by taking on a project that demands something of you.

BREATHING AND LEARNING

Your brain consumes 20% of your total oxygen intake. Anything you can do to increase the quality of the oxygen that gets to your brain will increase your mental effectiveness. Chapter 8 addresses this in depth. However, breathing is discussed here because it plays a particularly important role in the learning process. Consider the words of Ostrander and Schroeder from their book, *Superlearning*: "We seldom give breathing much attention, yet we breathe about 5,000 gallons (35 pounds) of air every day, about six times our food and drink consumption." They point out that when breathing to a regular beat, as opposed to haphazardly, your mind sharpens automatically.

If you retain your breath for a few seconds between breaths, mental activity stabilizes and the mind can focus in on a single point or idea. To varying degrees, the movement of breath is the movement of consciousness.

MUSIC AND LEARNING

In *Superlearning*, Ostrander and Schroeder state that, "a continuous, monotonous rhythm of somewhere around ten seconds seems to open up the mind's ability to remember." Classical music from the baroque period is widely believed the most effective music for this purpose. The precise rhythm of baroque music promotes a sense of well-being and relaxed receptivity.

Large music stores have such huge selections of classical music, the biggest stumbling block for me was figuring out which music to purchase. I've been pleased with a ten CD set I purchased from Costco for $30 called "Baroque Treasuries". This set is distributed by Delta Music, Inc. (310-826-6151). It contains music by Vivaldi, Bach, Handel, Teleman, Corelli and others. The following movements appear representative of the type of music suggested by the literature. The CD index numbers correspond to the 1990 version of this CD set:

CD	Concerto	Movement	#
Vivaldi: The Four Seasons	Concerto No. 4 in E minor, RV 297, "Winter"	Largo	11
Baroque Highlights		Handel: Largo (from Xerxes) Budapest Strings	2
Handel: Music For The Royal Fireworks	Concerto grosso in B flat, Op. 3 No. 2	Largo	16

I'd appreciate hearing about any selections that you have found useful (mir@bdance.com).

When being exposed to new material, I find it helpful to use these breathing and music techniques to help keep me relaxed, and even distract my conscious mind a bit during the initial stages of the learning process. These ideas come from the field of "Accelerated Learning" which I have not been able to research fully. Interested readers are encouraged to read *Accelerated Learning* by Colin Rose for more information.

SUMMARY OF KEY DISTINCTIONS REGARDING INFORMATION MANAGEMENT

- **Clarity.** As the amount of information expands, there is an increasing need for clarification of the exact type of information you are looking for. "Your results will depend upon your clarity." Clarity is power, and it becomes more powerful as available information resources expand. As described in Chapter 2, the "solutions approach" is based on the realization that the subconscious mind is the ultimate information filter. Emerson's statement "Do the thing and you shall have the power" can be interpreted as "Do the thing and you will be directed to and made aware of the information you need to do it."

- **Selectivity.** As the amount of information increases in a given area, there is an increasing need to scan that information at a high level and to be very selective of the areas you choose to study in detail.

- **Structure:** *As the amount of information you have to deal with increases, there is an increasing need for structure in order to avoid decisional stress.* Information tends to expand choices. Careful decisions made up front and occasionally reviewed about the way information will be processed can increase our capacity to handle information. Oftentimes this means consistency (i.e. putting things in the same place; deciding on information flow handling rules ahead of time, so you don't have to think about how to organize something every time).

- **Capacity/Awareness Link.** Our awareness of information tends to expand to meet our capacity to use information. Doing something to increase your information handling capacity will tend to expand the amount of information you are aware of. As mentioned

before, buying a new bookshelf, filing cabinet, a larger
hard disk or implementing a new system for managing
the flow ideas in your life can have this effect. In Aldous
Huxley's words, "Knowledge is a function of being.
When there is a change in the being of the knower,
there is a corresponding change in the nature and
amount of knowledge."

- **Context.** Our interaction with information is context
  driven. If you want to expand your awareness and
  understanding of certain information, then give yourself
  a reason to do so. Take on a project or set a goal that
  creates a context within which that information could
  be applied.

- **80/20 Rule.** The Perato principle applies to information
  interaction in that 80% of the value comes from 20% (or
  less) of the information. Which 20% depends on the
  specific outcome you are trying to create. When you
  begin to solve problems associated with creating a
  particular outcome, questions arise. Those questions
  direct your attention towards the high leverage
  information.

- **Meta-information.** Meta-information is information
  about the structure of ideas within a title or database.
  Information about the way the ideas relate to each
  other is often highly useful, but often not easily
  extracted from text presented in a linear fashion.

- **Compound Knowledge.** Knowledge in a particular
  field compounds just as investment interest does. The
  more you know, the easier it is to acquire new ideas.
  The more knowledge you transfer into long term
  memory, the more effective your subsequent learning
  efforts will be. When you read the next book on the
  topic, you can skip over material you already know.
  This distinction helps me plow through the early stages
  of the learning cycle where the knowledge compounds at
  slower rates—I know things will be much different
  when I get to the steep part of the curve.

- **Masters.** In most fields of inquiry, there are usually individuals or businesses who have reached a level of mastery far beyond average—who are very high on the compound learning curve. The critical mass these masters have built often makes them the premier center for useful distinctions in their area. W. Edwards Deming (total quality management), Milton Erickson (hypnotherapy), and Stephen Covey (self-development) are a few good examples.

- **Profound Knowledge**. One reward of exploring the world of self-improvement is when you discover an idea that has a positive impact on many areas of your life. I think this is what Dr. W. Edwards Deming meant by the term, "profound knowledge". For example, an idea that increases the amount of physical and mental energy available to you by 20% not only improves how you feel during the day, it can also increase the rate at which you acquire new information, including additional distinctions about how to increase your energy even more.

- **Ultimate Information Appliance.** The personal computer is to our mind's ability to process information what the phone is to our ears, the TV is to our eyes, and what the car is to our legs. Computers amplify our ability to interact with information. They have both accelerated the information explosion and provided us with a means of managing the resulting infoglut.

- **Rarity of Information.** The value of information is often in opposite proportion to the number of people who are aware of it.

- **Monetary Value of Information.** "Where there are economic interests, there is often valuable information," teaches Richard Schaffer, member of the National Speakers Association. In *"The Art of Strategic Planning for Information Technology"*, Bernard Boar writes: "What everyone knows has already happened. What everyone knows is not called wisdom. What the aware individual knows is what has not yet taken shape; what has not yet occurred." The idea is to "see the subtle and notice the hidden so as to seize victory when there is no form."

- **Current Information.** The most current information is usually in the minds of people who are actually doing the work—solving business problems or conducting the research. When a person takes the time to write their discoveries in language others can understand, it takes away from time they could be using to conduct further experiments. Some things are very easy to do, and difficult to explain in written or linear form. Some information is best transferred intuitively, by just being in someone's presence while they are "in the act". On the other hand, some ideas are best mastered through the investment in mental clarity it takes to teach them to others, which is another reason I'm writing this book.

- **Information Acquisition Does Not Equal Learning.** Learning has only occurred when you have increased your capacity for effective action in some area. Attempting to learn by simply acquiring information rather than doing is analogous to furnishing a room by throwing wood, metal, cotton, cloth, nails, etc. into an empty room. You have all of the components used in dressers, beds and chairs, but they are not organized in a meaningful or useful way.

- **Active Information vs. Interesting Information.** Richard Bandler was right on when he said, "The only kind of understanding that I'm interested in is the kind that allows you to do something." So much of what we read is merely "interesting", but does nothing to help us decide what to do differently as a result of reading it. Sort incoming information by usefulness.

- **Information Value/Usefulness Link**. The value of information is based upon its usefulness, which is determined by your current objectives. Peter Drucker tells us, "The greatest wisdom not applied to action and behavior is meaningless data." There is so much information available to us in any given situation that to pay attention to irrelevant information is to risk rendering yourself ineffective. Just as Eskimos have many words for snow because it is all around them, having several words for information may help prevent us from being "snowed under" by infoglut. Below is an attempt to categorize the ways I use information in knowledge work.

- **Strategic** – Useful in formulating strategic plans— making high level directional decisions.
- **Product** – Can be built into a product and thus sold to others. The Japanese have excelled in their emphasis on information which can be built into products and sold to other nations.
- **Project** – Information that will help you complete whatever project you are working on.
- **Emotional** – That which inspires you to action you would not have otherwise taken. This type of information is valuable to the extent that it generates action-oriented emotions within you. It doesn't relate to any one task, it just increases your motivation to complete the task.
- **Process** – Information that allows you to refine the processes you use to perform strategically important activities.
- **Systems** – Information about how changes in one area impact other aspects of a system. Information that helps you identify high leverage changes within an overall system.
- **Structural** – Information about the structure of information, or in the case of on-line information, how to search or filter the information. An example of how to think structurally is given in the use of mindmaps as a note-taking tool. Mindmaps help you to see how ideas in the book relate to each

other by mapping out the overall structure at a
high level.

CONCLUSION

Conscious ⟷ Subconscious

Individual Thought ⟷ Dialogue

Left-Brain Mode ⟷ Right-Brain Mode

Detailed Thought ⟷ High Level Thought

This chapter addressed the fourth major strategy for
employing complementary opposite modes of thinking:
traversing the structure of our thoughts in order to optimize
important mental processes. There are countless other ways
of applying the idea of complementary opposites, some of
which are mentioned in the remaining chapters. I
emphasized these four because they have been the most
useful in my work.

The next chapter will examine methods of applying these
distinctions towards a topic of increasing importance in our
lives: mastering the ultimate information appliance.

CHAPTER 7

MASTERING THE ULTIMATE INFORMATION APPLIANCE

"The computer has both created the information explosion and given us the means of managing it."

— *Paul Zane Pilzer*

The computer is to our mind what the car is to our legs, the phone is to our ears and the TV is to our eyes—it amplifies our capacity to interact with information. The personal computers (PCs) of today do far more than "compute". They are the fundamental tool for managing infoglut in the information age. It is often said that if the auto industry did what the computer industry has done over the past few decades, a Rolls Royce would cost less than $2 and get over 100,000 miles to the gallon. Bill Gates' 3/16/95 column in the Wall Street Journal stated that the price of computing has dropped by more than a factor of 100,000 in the past 20 years. With Intel Corporation highly focused on the herculean task of doubling the number of circuits on a chip every 18 months, this trend is likely to continue. This means that software will get easier to use and existing software will run faster. Faster software means that the investment you make today to learn software will reap increasing benefits.

In most cases, mastering an information appliance involves mastering software. Therefore, the main focus of this chapter is how the ideas presented thus far in Brain Dancing can be applied to the process of learning software faster.

Learning software is an art. By adding the following learning strategies to your toolbox, you will be able to respond more flexibly to the unique learning situations you come across.

➜   Large software programs are essentially a collection of highly organized information. There are two basic ways of interacting with this information: as a wandering generality, or in a highly focused manner with a specific project in mind. I use both approaches, but am careful to limit the orientation (wandering generality) phase by setting fixed time limits for this type of learning, and by finding a project in which I can apply the software as soon as possible.

ORIENTATION PHASE

This is the high level scan of the "information lake", using the metaphor established in Chapter 6. Begin this scan by looking at every page of printed documentation at the rate of one page per second. Put Post-it note tabs on any page that is obviously highly useful.

As mentioned in the previous chapter, it often helps to be relaxed both mentally and physically while scanning this material. Breathe rhythmically, retaining the breath for a few moments as you scan. If possible, put on some baroque music while orienting yourself to the material.

After installing the software, open up all sample files (documents, spreadsheets, databases, etc.) provided with the product, and flip through the screens of text or data at the rate of one screen per second. Use the sample files to select every menu option and icon to see what they do.

This high-level review helps eliminate the fear of the unknown and gives you an idea where significant functionality can be found. When novice software users get stuck, they are often hesitant to select menu options that haven't been tried before. They sit and wonder what to do rather than just looking around and trying things that seem appropriate. This hesitancy appears to be based on a fear of the unknown and fear of making mistakes which could cause data loss. Eliminating hesitancy is discussed further in the "What-if Learning" section.

INFORMATION SOURCE MINDMAP

➔   During the orientation phase, I sometimes create a mindmap of available information sources such as the following:

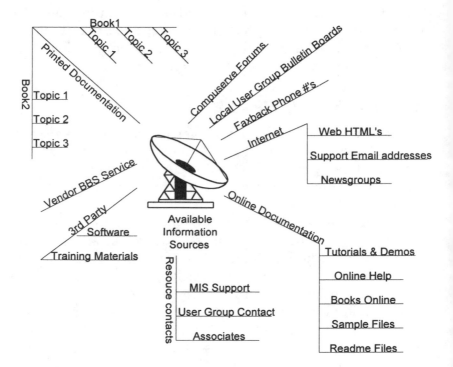

Mindmaps work well for this because it is easy to add new information as it becomes available. I refer to this mindmap when I'm immersed in the details of solving a problem and get stuck. When working at the detail level, it is sometimes difficult to remember all the places I can turn for assistance. Creating this mindmap also encourages me to invest time up front identifying all available information sources.

INCUBATION: PUT TIME ON YOUR SIDE

When it looks like I'll be needing to learn a new software package, I invest some time right away orienting myself to the software, even if it is just five minutes. When I get back to the software two weeks or even two months later, my mind has already seen and had time to think about (incubate) the ideas. The more substantial the software and the more complex the underlying concepts, the more helpful it is to employ the incubation strategy.

Use spaced repetition to give your mind several passes over the material from multiple angles. For example, in one study session I might scan all printed documentation and go through the tutorial. The next day, week or month, depending upon the situation, I'll go through a book that employs a "hands-on" approach and take a walk through the building of a sample application or document. The next learning pass might involve scanning the sample applications or documents provided with the software or obtained from associates.

CONCEPT AND TERMINOLOGY MINDMAP

My experience suggests that learning software rarely involves memorizing lists of things. Instead, as software is used to solve problems, the information provided on screen becomes enough to jog the memory, one step at a time, towards the desired outcome.

However, most software comes with its own paradigm involving unique terminology and concepts. It is helpful to identify these up front and review them periodically to transfer them solidly into long-term memory. This review process can be facilitated by using a yellow highlighter in the manuals or by noting them in an "ongoing" mindmap. By ongoing, I mean that ideas are added as they come up in both the orientation and project learning phases.

As discussed in Chapter 6, review periods of 2-5 minutes should be completed ten minutes, 24 hours, one week, and one month after first learning the material. This mindmap

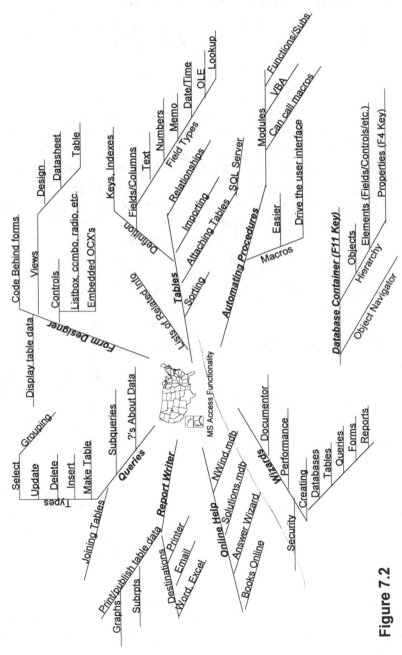

Figure 7.2

can be used with the visualization plus articulation strategy discussed in that chapter.

SOFTWARE OVERVIEW MINDMAP

→ Another activity I have found useful when dealing with software that has substantial functionality and is fairly new to me is to create a mindmap of the overall structure of the software. It delineates the major components and how they relate to each other. Figure 7.2 is an example of what this might look like for the Windows 95 version of Microsoft Access (relational database software).

Those of you familiar with Microsoft Access will notice many features have been omitted from this mindmap. To include them all would require a much larger piece of paper. The benefit comes more from the process of creating the mindmap than the end result. The mindmap you create will probably more closely reflect your situation (i.e., context). For example, novice computer users would probably emphasize more of the interactive features of Access, while more technically inclined users would probably include more information related to programming.

The process of creating this mindmap will encourage you to think about the software at "meta" levels. It will help reduce the chance of overlooking a key feature of the software that could save you tons of time (like the Database Wizard).

ACTIVE VS. PASSIVE LEARNING

It is one thing to know which keys to press and quite another to have the ability to create elegant and useful applications or documents with that software. While knowledge can be acquired by dabbling here and there, the development of software skills is best achieved by applying the tool to real world business problems.

After the initial overview, I go back to tutorials and walk-throughs that provide opportunities for active learning (i.e., exercises where *I* do the typing). A key objective is to build confidence in my ability to solve problems with the software.

This objective is supported when I know every keystroke and mouse click that goes into creating the application or document. When completed, these applications form good starting points for "what-if" learning experiments.

First hand knowledge is several times more effective at building capacity than second hand knowledge obtained by passively reading articles about other peoples' opinions. Both are useful, but time allocations should reflect this distinction.

SETTING UP A LEARNING JOURNAL

→   After creating all of these mindmaps, the question arises: Where do you put them? When learning any significant piece of software that I expect to use extensively, I create a three-ring notebook for organizing the information stream with the following sections:

| To Do's | Summaries | ?'s | Sample Apps | Journal |

- **To Do's:** Contains my learning plan. When I have time to study the software, notes that I've made in this section ahead of time allow me to get right to work.
- **Summaries:** This is where the above-mentioned mindmaps go.
- **?'s:** Recording unanswered questions as they arise frees me to move on to other issues. Many of these potential stumbling blocks get answered as I'm addressing other areas.
- **Sample Apps:** "Post-mortem" type information from applications I create. This includes data structure diagrams (discussed later), printouts of key routines (programs) that I used, etc. It may also contain listings of sample applications available from on-line information services and the Internet.
- **Learning Journal:** This "everything else" reference section contains material organized chronologically that I don't expect to use that often.

Any document in this binder that I expect to reference frequently gets its own yellow Post-it note tab. Take about ten 2"x1.5" yellow Post-it notes, cut them in half, and paste them on the back of the original pad. I keep these everywhere I learn and work, and even carry them in my DAY-TIMER. I usually stick a dozen blank tabs on the inside cover of the journal when I set it up. These tabs go along the top of the sheets so they don't block my view of the main tabs along the right border.

This journal is not an excuse to print reams of paper. As much information as possible is stored electronically so that it can be searched more efficiently.

FIGURE OUT WHAT NOT TO DO

➜ Another way to minimize hesitancy is to invest time up front figuring out what NOT to do. It is much easier to explore the user interface freely and experiment somewhat haphazardly when you are not working on live data.

Most quality software will give you a warning before letting you do something destructive. So when the software asks you to confirm an action, PAY ATTENTION!

I heard of one case where an individual could have benefited from this one. Records were mysteriously disappearing from the database. As it turned out, when this individual wanted to print the screen, he would press the "Delete" key. When asked if he was sure he wanted to delete the record, he selected "Yes," thinking, "Yes, I want to print the screen," and the record was deleted.

Be Extra Cautious with Shared Data! If your computer is hooked up to a corporate network, then extra caution is warranted. There is a big difference between experimenting with a spreadsheet calculation and trying new queries on your company's accounting database. When in doubt, ask an MIS support person: "I want to do some learning experiments. Are there any precautionary measures I should take while using this software?" or, "How can I set up my machine so that I can do some learning experiments without affecting anyone else's work?"

PROJECT PHASE: SKILL VS. KNOWLEDGE

Set an overall time limit for the orientation phase and find an opportunity to apply the software to a real-world problem as soon as you can. This is where the "solutions approach" discussed in Chapter 2 comes in. When applying software to a real-world problem, there are two sets of issues that must be addressed:

- Issues that define *what* the problem is or what the software must do to effectively solve the problem.
- Information about the *how* the software tool can be applied to meet that need. This is mostly technical details about how the software works.

One of the best ways I've found to simplify the software learning process is to team up with someone (ideally a client who will pay me) who will focus on the "what" side of this equation. I usually refer to this as the "business analyst" role. They don't need to know that much about computers, but they must thoroughly understand the business problem to be addressed. This understanding must include the boundary conditions which must be met in order to increase the business's ability to deliver value to its customers. This team approach also forms the basis for "synergistic dialogue" as discussed in Chapter 4.

In situations where such a team strategy doesn't apply, similar benefits can be obtained by using the software for something you already do manually or already know very well. In that case, the "what" has already been clearly defined.

If this strategy does not apply, then invest time creating a project specification that clearly delineates the "what" side of the equation. Make the first phase very simple, and use idea collection sheets to accumulate ideas for future versions. The specification gives you a clear target to hit and helps build confidence with the new tool. Without such a target, it is easy to get diverted by new possibilities. This increases the likelihood that you will end up with a bunch of features that don't work very well, and your self-confidence will not be increased.

Chapter 2 described several strategies for transitioning into new technologies. The most useful is probably the "incremental" strategy. This involves working on projects involving a combination of existing expertise and the new technology. People you have done work for in the past and who know your work ethic are more likely to trust you in getting the job done with new technology.

The following material elaborates on ideas presented in Chapter 2 as they apply to learning software.

THE 80/20 RULE

→   Using software for any one application often requires the use of a small percentage of the software's features. Perato's 80/20 rule is applicable here as well—80% of the value comes from 20% of the features. Stated another way, we often spend most of our time working with a small percentage of the features. When learning a new software program, your highest leverage learning time is what you invest in this core 20%. The challenge for most beginners is figuring out what questions to ask—that is, until they start working on a project.

When you start to apply the tool to a real-world business problem, all kinds of questions come up. These questions zero you right in on the core 20% of the software. In answering these questions, not only do you learn things likely to help you on the next project, but the current project serves as a metaphor for future reference—"When I needed to do 'X' on that other project, I used 'Y' approach."

METHODOLOGY

Another aspect of developing the capacity for skilled software application has to do with the process used to apply the tool—the methodology. Methodology is about doing the right things in the right sequence: begin with the end in mind, developing the skill of clarifying exactly what the end should be, knowing what pieces of the puzzle to build first, knowing when to stop tinkering, etc.

One of the best ways to learn methodology is to observe or talk to others who've done it before. In some cases this might involve attending user group meetings, hiring a consultant for a couple of hours, or just buying a friend lunch. Watching an expert at work can greatly accelerate your software learning, for even the most eloquent words pale in comparison to the information presented to us by our senses.

OTHER IDEAS FOR ACCELERATING SOFTWARE LEARNING

INVEST IN THE BEST

If you place a reasonable value on your time, then you will probably invest far more in learning a software package than the cost to acquire it. Learning time can be reduced when you purchase high quality software engineered for ease of use.

Every software program has its little quirks, shortcuts, etc., that once learned, add up to an ability to produce effective results with that package. The better the software, the less learning time you will have to invest, and the more value you will receive, in terms of capacity, for the time you do invest.

When you purchase software, you are investing in an information stream from the software manufacturer. When making a software decision, ask yourself if the work demonstrates innovation skills likely to result in a stream of high quality state of the art upgrades.

The late Don Estridge, who played a key role in the creation and launch of the original IBM PC in 1981, summed up IBM's research this way: "What we discovered was that the way people responded emotionally to PC's was more important than what the computer actually did."

Notice your emotional reaction to the software. Is it enjoyable to work with? Does it inspire ideas for new ways of applying the technology? Great software can be empowering, in that it enables you to do things that heretofore may have been impractical.

WHAT-IF LEARNING

➔ What-if learners know to experiment when they get stuck. Rather than staring at the screen wondering what might happen if they tried something, they know when it is safe to just try it. What-if experiments lead to further experiments, which often lead to the solution. In addition, they round out your knowledge of the overall product.

Do everything possible to eliminate hesitancy. Invest some time during the orientation phase discovering what not to do. Here are three ways to help make it safe to do what-if learning:

- **Learn how to make quick backups.** By making a copy of the file you are working on before you do the experiment, you can easily revert back to where things were before doing the experiments. I set up a backup directory called "bu" beneath my working directory. I then periodically copy my files to this directory using a different file name each time. For example, I would copy a file called "chapter5.doc" to "bu\chapter5.211". The "211" tells me it was made on February 11. This allows me to revert back to where I was at several different points along the way. If you are hooked up to a network, periodically copy your files to another computer's hard disk. This way you won't lose your work completely if your computer fails.

- **Just don't save your changes.** Some software allows you to make changes in memory and only write them to disk when you tell it to. To use this approach, save your work before you make the change, try the experiment, and if it doesn't work, simply close the file and answer "NO" when it asks you if you want to save your changes. Also make sure to disable any auto-save options before relying on this approach.

- **Single screen experimentation.** You can start a new experiment file and copy in the data you need to test your idea. I call this "single screen" experimentation because I try to limit the entire experiment to a single screen of information. This allows me to see everything that is going on when I make a change and encourages me to focus on process, as opposed to content. Keep these small "learning applications" handy for future reference. When working on a live application, it might help to load your learning application to perform some quick experiments before applying the techniques to live data.

LINE UP A REFERENCE PERSON

When you get to the point where nothing you try produces the outcome you want, the more people you can call on for quick questions the better. Remember the story of the shutdown power plant that called in a retired engineer who quickly rectified the situation by tapping the right pipe.

Many times when learning to use a new software program, you get to a point where it's just not obvious what to do. It has nothing to do with intelligence, you are just missing a piece of information that may be fairly unique to your situation. Having quick access to several experts, such as product support lines, user group associates, company support staff, or friends, can often save you hours trying to figure out "where to tap".

PROCESS OPTIMIZATION: TYPING & MOUSE MOVEMENT

→ Typing is where the tire meets the road in using a computer. If you can double or triple your typing speed, it often translates into getting computer related work done two or three times faster. A simple way to improve your typing skills is to type in the letters of the alphabet five times as fast as you can. Then do it backwards as fast as you can a few times. Do this once or twice a day. Alternatively, you can type the following phrase, which contains every letter of the alphabet:

The quick brown fox jumps over the lazy dog.

After doing it a couple of times, you may want to close your eyes and visualize your hands moving across the keyboard as they strike each key.

With Microsoft Windows software, the second most frequently performed activity is moving the mouse. One way to optimize this process is to set mouse movement sensitivity to maximum and then get used to it. You want the slightest movement on the mouse pad to translate into the largest movement on the screen. This will result in substantially less hand and wrist movement over time.

In versions prior to Windows 95, this setting is adjusted by selecting the Control Panel icon in the Main group in Program Manager, and then selecting the Mouse icon. In the dialog box that appears, locate the Mouse Tracking Speed setting, move it to the fastest position, and save your changes by selecting the "OK" button. Windows 95 users can change this setting by selecting the Start button, selecting the Settings and Control Panel menu options, and selecting the Mouse icon in the window that appears.

With most software, it pays off to invest a little time memorizing keyboard shortcuts, which are often faster than using a mouse.

SET UP AN ELECTRONIC KNOWLEDGE BASE

→ Leaving reference information in electronic form is more efficient to search, and saves paper, trees and money. Therefore, I store as much information in electronic form as possible. There are two types of electronic information I use to complement the on-line documentation and knowledge bases provided by most software vendors: reference text files and sample applications.

A detailed discussion of how to set up and use an electronic knowledge base is beyond the scope of this book. The following discussion provides general guidelines and may require the assistance of someone with at least intermediate computer skills.

REFERENCE TEXT FILES

These are stored in a subdirectory I call "KB," which is placed directly beneath the main software directory. For example, a knowledge base for Corel Draw! would be placed in a directory called "c:\corel\kb". In this directory I store related Internet web pages, excerpts from Internet newsgroups or CompuServe message forums, and e-mail messages from mailing lists. All files in this directory are stored in ASCII text format. This enables me to use a text search utility to quickly scan every file in the directory for specific key words. While there are probably more user-friendly options available, I use the text search utility called "ts.exe," which is part of the Norton Utilities published by Symantec.

SAMPLE APPLICATIONS

Sample applications obtained from CompuServe, the Internet, or user group bulletin boards, are placed in a directory called "sampapps". Using the above example, the directory would be called "c:\corel\sampapps". Consistently using the same directory names gives me one less thing to decide or remember when learning each new software package.

SOFTWARE-SPECIFIC SUGGESTIONS

The preceding strategies are fairly generic and can be applied towards learning a variety of software packages. The following discussion narrows the focus a bit by describing specific techniques for getting the most out of the most popular types of software: spreadsheets, word processors, electronic mail and databases.

SPREADSHEETS

→ • Use block diagrams for depicting the overall layout of the spreadsheet. This is especially helpful when studying a file created by someone else, or when managing an especially large spreadsheet. I use these less often now that tabbed workbooks are available.

Summary
Sales
Expenses

• The best spreadsheets come from the best manual systems. In the early days when I did spreadsheet consulting, I had the good fortune of working with a few companies who had thought out manual spreadsheets to the *nth* degree. They would hand me an 11x17 columnar worksheet crammed with numbers and ask me to create its electronic equivalent. These were the most successful applications I did. Other, less organized clients taught me the truth of the adage: "Sometimes when you automate a mess, you just end up doing the wrong things faster."

• Don't make them so complex that you don't understand what's happening with the numbers. When a spreadsheet becomes so complex that management views it as a "black box", its usefulness is compromised.

Spreadsheet technology gives us so much computational power that it is easy to get carried away in its application.

- Just one number can throw the calculations off significantly. While working on a very large and complex spreadsheet created by someone else, we found an error in a single row altered the bottom line by over $1 billion. Admittedly, this was a very long term forecast, but it emphasized the importance of keeping spreadsheets as simple as possible in order to minimize the chances of this happening.

- Forecasts are just forecasts. You still have to make them happen. When I hear stories about forecasts concerning our national debt and deficit, I am reminded that creating a brilliantly architected spreadsheet with every formula perfect is no substitute for brilliant execution. This is especially true with sales numbers, which often have the greatest impact on the bottom line.

- Explore Microsoft Excel's pivot tables or Lotus Improv for some innovative enhancements of PC technology that aren't as widely appreciated as they should be.

WORD PROCESSORS

- Try writing in different fonts or varying the margin widths for overcoming writer's block. For some reason, I do my best writing when working with columns 4-5 inches wide.

- When writing creatively, it is critical that you minimize mental bandwidth allocated to form as opposed to content. You want to get the content in and organized as fast as possible. Only when this is done do I worry about format. Microsoft Word has a feature called style sheets which can make revising the appearance of your documents a breeze.

- Integrated outline processors such as the one provided with Microsoft Word assist in the process of "going meta". They allow you to quickly switch between a detailed view of your document and a high level outline. On large monitors, an outline view of the same document can be placed alongside your typing window. This helps me write individual sections with the overall context in mind.
- Separate the writing and editing phases. One sure way to cure this problem is to write your first draft on paper, and then type it into your word processor for editing. I am often amazed at how I can express ideas better in handwritten form than I can in front of the keyboard. However, the more I practice, the better I'm getting at doing my first draft on the computer as well.

E-MAIL

- In an interview with New Yorker magazine, Bill Gates indicated that he spends about 2 hours per day reading and responding to e-mail. With all of the demands placed upon his time, what does that tell you about the potential value of e-mail? According to the article, Gates uses all lowercase and minimizes the use of social nicetics for increased efficiency.
- E-mail can increase the information metabolism of a company by minimizing the overhead associated with an information exchange event. The less time it takes to exchange information, the more likely you are to do it, and the more your company can accomplish in less time.
- A study done by Wanda Orlikowski at the MIT Sloan School of Management points out that not only must peoples' mental models appreciate the potential of groupware, but "...where the premises underlying the groupware technology (shared effort, cooperation, collaboration) are counter-cultural to an organization's structural properties (competitive and individualistic

culture, rigid hierarchy, etc.), the technology will be unlikely to facilitate collective use and value."[12] If everyone on the team is not committed to checking their e-mail periodically throughout the day and responding promptly, team members are less likely to use e-mail. You have to trust that once sent, the other person will both receive and read the message in a timely manner. The next time you upgrade your computer, consider keeping the old one around as an e-mail machine. This allows you to check e-mail with just a glance, vs. starting the software each time, or tying up memory on your main computer by leaving it running.

DATABASE SOFTWARE

Most company information is stored in relational databases. Do whatever it takes to learn how to read data structure diagrams such as the one shown in Figure 7.3. While they are not that complex, many users seem intimidated by them, or just don't understand their value. These diagrams represent on a single page, the most useful information available about what and how data is stored in a database. When this understanding is combined with an ability to use a query engine such as those included with Borland's Paradox or Microsoft Access, you will be able to ask a vast array of questions about any database with a relatively small amount of effort.

Here is a brief introduction to data structure diagrams using the "Ledger" application generated by the Microsoft Access 95 Database Wizard.

The data structure diagram in Figure 7.3 shows that this database application contains three tables: Transactions, Accounts and Account Types. The Transactions table is nothing more than an electronic check register. The Accounts table describes how the checks are to be categorized, and the

---

[12] Wanda J. Orlikowski, WP #3428-92, CCS TR No. 131, MIT Sloan School of Management, Cambridge, MA.

Account Types table describes how Accounts are categorized. As indicated by the arrows, the Transactions and Accounts tables are linked by the AccountID field, and the Accounts and Account Types tables are linked by the AccountTypeID field.

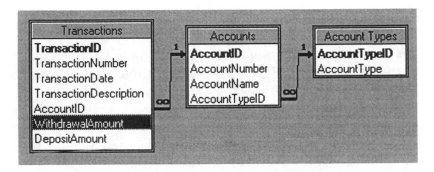

Figure 7.3 Simple Data Structure Diagram.

Accounts : Table			
Account ID	**Account Number**	**Account Name**	**Account Type**
1	610	Meals	1
2	620	Transportation	1
3	630	Lodging	1
4	640	Miscellaneous	1
5	410	Rental Income	2
6	650	Power Bill	1

Figure 7.4 Corresponding "Accounts" Table.

Account Types : Table	
Account Type ID	**Account Type**
1	Expenses
2	Revenues
3	Liabilities
4	Other

Figure 7.5 Corresponding "Account Types" Table.

Ok, what do I mean by "linked together" and "field". As you can see in Figures 7.4 and 7.5, a table consists of rows of information divided into columns. Each column is called a field. These tables are linked based on the "AccountTypeID" field. The "Rental Income" account has been assigned an AccountTypeID of 2.

If you look in the Account Types table, you can see that an AccountTypeId of 2 corresponds to an account type of "Revenues". When two tables are "linked" by a field, it means that the data contained in a field in one table corresponds to a row in the other table.

Understanding the above data structure diagram makes it very easy to use a query tool to ask questions such as: "What were my total deposits and withdrawals for each account type or account number?"

Yes, I've simplified things to the nth degree here. Yes, this section may take a little more study than most in this book. But keep in mind that this is a powerful set of ideas with broad application in business. Its well worth your effort to learn how to read a data structure diagram. In larger databases, the number of tables and lines will be greater, but many of these basic ideas are equally applicable.

PERSONAL ECOLOGY

For many knowledge workers, PCs are a means and not an end. Therefore, it is essential that knowledge workers not allow their software learning efforts to divert them from their primary area of specialized knowledge—that which they get paid for.

I know highly successful business people who know very little about PCs. They are very good at what they do and have developed systematic strategies for consistently delivering value to their customers. Taking time to flip through computer manuals trying to figure out what keys to press is a diversion from their "master strategy". For them, investing the time to learn about computers has been risky to the extent that it required so much time and mental energy, it diverted them from the skillful and consistent implementation of their master plan.

I believe that fear of diversion is a primary reason many people have put off learning to use computers. The key is to set a fixed time limit on the amount of time you will spend each week learning the software, and then stick to that time limit.

PCs are getting easier to use, and the breadth of applications is expanding rapidly. The ratio of value received per minute invested learning is increasing, making PCs an even greater means of achieving mental leverage.

CHAPTER 8

OPTIMIZING MENTAL CLARITY

"The secret to effective systems development of any kind, manual or automated, is clear logical thinking and expression—everything else is secondary."

— *Ken Orr*

➜ "More coals!" shouted Anthony Robbins. I was standing barefoot in front of a twelve foot bed of coals burning between 600 and 2000 degrees Fahrenheit. After doing my first couple power moves, "Whooossshhh!!" "BOOOOOOOOMM!!" Robbins wanted his assistant to add a little more fuel to the fire.

Two more shovels full of smoldering coals burning bright yellow-orange in the dark night did not sway my determination to walk. I cranked my energy level up another few notches with two more power moves: "Whooossshhh!!" "BOOOOOOOOMM!!"

My energy level exploded past "level 10", and this time Robbins gave me the go-ahead: "You're ready," he said. A few seconds later I was safely across—one of nearly 300 people who walked that night in 1988 at the Museum of History and Industry in Seattle.

Before continuing, I want to make it very clear that I am in no way recommending that you do a firewalk. If,

however, you ever find yourself considering a firewalk, make sure you do it with the guidance of a professional trainer with a proven track record. Improperly performed firewalks can be extremely dangerous!

My feet tingle as I write, several years later, just as they have every time I've ever shared this story with others. "Crazy!" you say? Well, that's what I would have thought before that night. In fact, I wasn't planning on walking. After studying the cutting edge material in Robbins' *Unlimited Power* book and audiotapes, I knew I could learn plenty just by listening. Besides, I had done my research before attending: Robbins' Research sales staff told me that of 89,000 people who had done firewalks prior to this event, eleven had been burned seriously enough to be hospitalized. Apparently two of these eleven people had actually died from complications resulting from the burns![13]

That was all the information I needed—no way was I going to walk. Yes, the odds were pretty small, but the downside risk seemed pretty high! That night, Robbins gave an absolutely incredible presentation. He also made the risks of walking very clear to the audience. This was not brainwashing, it was an opportunity for personal growth for those willing to "stretch". When the group headed for the coals, I went along and even got in line at the coals for a brief moment. I remember thinking that this could really put a damper on my upcoming snow skiing plans—that was all the reason I needed to get out of there.

Always in "constant learn mode", I realized that this was a great opportunity to study the others who were walking. So I walked around and stood two feet from the side of the coals as others walked across. Person after person walked

---

[13] My initial impression was that these injuries occured at Robbins Research seminars. However, during his November, 1995 *"Empowernet"* seminar, Robbins stated that none of these eleven people were burned during one of his firewalks.

successfully, including a 70 year old man, and with some special assistance, an 11 year old boy.

Robbins' words began to re-play in my head: "If you can't, then you must! And if you must, then you can!" In other words, if you know you can safely do something, and if you were to do it, it would help you reach farther towards your true potential, then if you don't follow through, you are living a life of limitation, cheating yourself and everyone around you. We are all on our own personal development path. Something inside told me that there was an important lesson I could learn by walking. Yes, it was risky, and I'd just seen over 200 people walk successfully, including a friend I'd known for almost 20 years. This was no illusion. If I followed the guidelines prescribed, this was something I could safely perform. So back in line I went, and I'm extremely glad that I did. I feel a deep sense of gratitude to Anthony Robbins for creating this learning opportunity.

In addition to learning how to break through limiting fears and take action, one of the most important lessons wrapped up in this experience was this: your energy level is not something that just happens to you—that would make us all puppets. Energy is something you can create within yourself on demand if you know the "levers". Every technique presented in this book requires energy both to understand and to apply. This chapter is about the metaskill of being able to cultivate high levels of personal energy. I gave this chapter the title "Optimizing Mental Clarity" to emphasize a significant side benefit I experience while doing things to increase my natural energy level. The quality of my thinking improves and I have more mental energy to apply to each moment of my life. I am able to work longer hours without getting tired and I get more done during the time I work. When I spend time with my family, this energy allows me to give more of myself in these moments as well.

Contrast your thinking at peak mental alertness with the experience of doing thought intensive work after a large heavy lunch. When the mind is clear, ideas come more easily, thoughts are formulated faster with greater precision, and communication with others is more effective. Within three months of completing Robbins' seminar, my income doubled to over $8,000 per month. One year after that I "imploded," and that's why Chapter 9 is about personal ecology.

The self-development field is loaded with great ideas, many of which could be addressed in this chapter. However, the emphasis of this book has been to point you in directions most likely to yield the highest leverage—the most benefit per minute of time invested. With this in mind, I've devoted the first half of this chapter to the topic of juicing. This is followed by an overview of several other key distinctions that you may want to explore.

Time you invest now to learn new distinctions for cultivating personal energy will benefit you for the rest of your life, to the extent that you apply them wisely. This topic more than any other has the potential to impact every other area of your life. More energy means more energy for learning, and because learning compounds over a lifetime, it can accelerate your journey on this compound learning curve.

JUICING: THE ULTIMATE SUPPLEMENT

We are constantly participating in a "dance of life" which involves continual give and take throughout nature. Try taking a breath with the realization that you are inhaling oxygen produced by vegetation somewhere on the planet. You are nourishing your cells with their exhalation of oxygen, and when you exhale, you give back to the environment nutrients plants use to sustain their existence. We owe our lives to plants not only for the oxygen they create, but also for the nutrients they extract from the soil and store in their roots and leaves.

Juicing is the process of using a juice extractor to separate the juice of fruits and vegetables from the fiber. You drink the juice and discard the fiber. Chewing, swallowing, digesting, assimilating—this entire process is aimed at one end—extracting nutrients from food in a way that your body can assimilate them into your blood stream, and thus circulate them throughout the body to nourish your cells. The human body is a juice extractor! Juicing removes the burden of the first three steps from your body. This frees up energy that can be used for other things.

Juicing does not replace the need to eat! It can reduce the amount you need to eat since your body doesn't have to filter through as much "bulk" in order to sift out the essential nutrients it needs. This is why I refer to juicing as the ultimate supplement, it amplifies your in-take of high quality nutrients directly from the source—Mother Nature.

If you have ever put Miracle Grow on plants and watched them burst with new growth and larger healthier produce, then you understand the basic concept behind drinking freshly prepared juices.

For myself and other "juicers" I've observed, new activities began to blossom in our lives. For example, I know a restaurant owner who feels that juicing gave him the boost he needed to dust off his magic act. As a result, now hundreds of people fill high school gymnasiums to enjoy this magical entertainment that has been dormant for years.

As with any significant change in your dietary patterns, you are advised to seek the advise of a medical doctor knowledgeable in nutritional matters or other professional nutritionist before beginning to juice. This is especially important if you have any history of blood sugar disorders such as diabetes or hypoglycemia.

Personally, I've implemented so many lifestyle changes to improve my health and energy, that it is hard to know which ones were responsible for the benefits I've received. In truth, it is probably all of them in combination. With this in mind, the most significant benefits I attribute at least in part to juicing are:

- Improves mental clarity. This helps me communicate more effectively with others. Clearer thinking helps me formulate thoughts and increases my level of awareness in conversations. It also increases the speed with which I can think.

- Increases mental and physical energy for learning new technologies and personal development distinctions.
- Improves overall health and strengthens my immune system.

I make no guarantees that you will experience similar results, since everyone is different in their nutritional needs.

WHICH CHEMIST DO YOU TRUST?

→   The two primary purposes of eating are:

1) To provide the necessary nutrients to our cells, and
2) To consume enough fiber to cleanse our intestinal tract.

People consume supplements because they believe that the quality of the material they consume will impact the quality of their health and energy. In the energy portion of my seminars, I hold up a plate of uncooked vegetables (carrots, kale, green bell pepper, etc.) in one hand, and rattle a bottle of vitamin pills in the other. I then ask the audience, "Which chemist do you trust more: the one who made these (referring to the plate of veggies), or the one who made these (rattling the bottle of pills)?"

Most people seem to get the point. The problem is that most of us don't have the time, energy or the teeth to chew and assimilate this much produce once or twice a day. The answer is not to eat them, but to drink them!

As the "Juiceman" Jay Kordach says, "Every fiber of our being is made from Earth, yet we cannot just reach down, take a handful of soil and consume it. We are totally dependent upon the plants to lower their roots into the soil, extract certain combinations of nutrients, and convert them into substances we can consume." Kordach encourages people to go directly to the source for nutrients as much as possible.

Late Breaking News: Just before going to press, I was reading *Smart Eating by* Covert Bailey. He points out that muscles not used tend to atrophy, and that this may also apply to our digestive system. The basic idea is that supplements make it so easy for the body to assimilate nutrients, that over time, the digestive system could become "lazy". There may be some truth to this, and I'd be interested in comparing notes with others on this issue via E-mail. It is all the more reason not to go overboard with juicing or vitamins. This may explain why I've developed the habit of nibbling on the produce as I prepare it for juicing.

One of the best ways I know to give my digestive system a healthy workout is to eat the following once a week:

1. Take a cup of organic short grain brown rice (you buy this in bulk from the health food store), about half as much organic hard red winter wheat, some olive oil, chop up a large carrot, some parsley, celery, mushrooms and a few cloves of garlic.
2. Put it all in a stir fry and pour in enough water to cover everything plus about a half inch.
3. Let it simmer for about 20 minutes, turn off the burner and let it sit for another 10 minutes.

Most of the water should be soaked up by the rice and it should be fairly tender. I sometimes add a little sea salt and unsalted butter for added flavor. This will make 2 or 3 meals and costs less than $2 to make.

Juicing is an experiment. The last word has not yet been written. I feel that the benefits I've received have been significant, but I must again encourage you to proceed with caution.

ENZYMES

➔   While enzymes are a fascinating subject, precise and consistent information on their role in digestion has been hard to come by. From what I've been able to learn so far, the enzyme theory goes something like this: raw food is alive and contains enzymes that assist the body in digesting and assimilating the food and nutrients therein. Cooking food diminishes the vitamin and mineral content and destroys the enzymes. This places the burden of generating enzymes on the pancreas. Not only does this require nerve energy, but over time it also begins to take its toll on the pancreas. I have no idea how difficult it is to "generate enzymes" at the molecular level, but it seems to make sense to give the pancreas all the help I can.

MAKING JUICING PRACTICAL FOR BUSY KNOWLEDGE WORKERS

With full acknowledgment that everyone is different in their nourishment needs, I will share with you the results of seven years of experimentation with juicing. The eleven guidelines for making juicing practical are:

1) Avoid synthetic vitamin A.
2) Trust your taste buds.
3) The 10 minute rule.
4) Once or twice a day consistently.
5) Carrot/apple base.
6) Emphasize vegetable juice.
7) Variety is key, so vary the remaining 25%.
8) Use organic produce as much as possible.
9) Drink juice immediately.
10) Juice on an empty stomach.
11) Feed your mind while you juice.

1) AVOID SYNTHETIC VITAMIN A

→ Avoid supplements with synthetic vitamin A or synthetic beta-carotene!!!!!!!. Some vitamins are fat soluble, which makes it difficult for your body to dispose of unused portions. They are vitamins A and E. I take a vitamin E supplement occasionally because it is difficult to obtain from food.

If your body is getting all of the vitamin A it needs from natural sources, the likelihood of toxic buildup in the body is significantly increased, and people have been known to die from such overdoses!

A friend of mine started juicing regularly while continuing to take a multi-vitamin containing synthetic vitamin A. On the positive side, juicing eliminated his need to take colitis medication. On the negative side, he soon began getting headaches, which his doctor told him was one symptom of vitamin A overdose.

This symptom can be misleading. Have you ever gotten so busy at work that you let your housecleaning go for a while and things sort of piled up? The same thing happens to your body when you eat in a way that causes it to work overtime. When a person begins to juice, nerve energy is freed up to do house cleaning that had been neglected due to other needs. This sometimes results in headaches and mucus until the cleansing is complete. I don't know how to tell the difference between a cleansing headache and a vitamin A overdose headache. All I can say is BE CAREFUL IF YOU GET HEADACHES after beginning to juice, and avoid synthetic vitamin A just to be safe.

As far as I can tell, you cannot overdose on natural sources of beta-carotene. Nevertheless, the adage "moderation in all things" seems prudent here as well. Carrots contain no vitamin A, only beta-carotene, which the body converts to vitamin A as needed. I've read or heard of people consuming one gallon of carrot juice per day for extended periods of time with no ill effects. However, common sense tells me to be careful here. "All excesses are ultimately their own undoing", to quote Paul Harvey. Our bodies have built-in warning systems which help us minimize the chances of consuming too much fresh juice, which leads us to guideline number 2...

2) TRUST YOUR TASTE BUDS

➔   I trust my "taste bud judgment" to know if my body needs the nutrients in the juice. If the juice tastes bad, I dump it out. I use a mental scale of 1 to 10, where 1 is lousy, 5 is neutral, and 10 is great. I dump any juice that registers below 4.

There is a larger issue involved here—that intelligence is distributed throughout the body. I'll bet most people have had the experience where even the thought of eating a certain food turned their stomach. Or maybe the odor of some food didn't pass the "smell test". What I didn't learn until recently, however, was that our ability to "tune-in" to this bodily intelligence is increased as we begin to detoxify our body. It may take some time to improve your "taste bud" awareness.

There are occasional times when carrot juice doesn't "sound" good to me. The thought of carrot juice makes my stomach turn. Rather than generalize that "I must not like carrot juice any more". I simply switch my dietary pattern for a day or four. Even more importantly, some days I'll make juice and take one sip only to find that it makes my stomach turn because it tastes bad. I trust that my taste buds are telling me either that I do not need the nutrients in the juice or that perhaps one of the ingredients used was spoiled. In either case, I do not hesitate to dump this juice down the drain, regardless of the cost or time invested to make it. When in doubt, throw it out.

The "taste bud" test is the key means of compensating for the fact that everyone is different. Specifically, our ancestral dietary patterns have impacted our body's capacity to assimilate nutrients from various sources. For example, some people are better equipped to handle the coarse proteins in dairy products. In addition to heredity differences, our bodies are a product of nature, and our body chemistry seems to fluctuate (i.e., to have internal seasons). Our taste buds seem to "know" what season it is internally and what food will provide the nutrients we need.

The "taste bud" principle is only meant to be applied to foods that our understanding and wisdom tell us should be good for us. In other words, some foods taste good but we know we would be better off not eating them (i.e., chocolate).

This informal agreement with my taste buds is an essential component of my strategy. It allows me to juice on a consistent basis, while others seem to lose interest in juicing after a month or two. Another key reason people lose interest in juicing is the time it takes, which leads us to the first of several strategies I have for minimizing the impact juicing has on my schedule.

3) THE 10 MINUTE RULE

The longer it takes to juice, the greater the likelihood that you won't do it consistently. Consequently, I do the following two things to keep the time it takes to juice—from preparation to consumption and cleanup—to under 10 minutes.

- Use a juicer that can be assembled and cleaned quickly.
- Systematize the process thereby minimizing the number of decisions required each time I juice.

Selecting a Juicer
The most important criteria are:
- Time to clean up.
- Nutrient extraction efficiency.
- Doesn't heat up & thus destroy life enhancing nutrients.
- Durable and reliable.
- Pulp free juice.
- Quantity of juice before jamming.
- Price.

My two favorite juicers are the Juiceman Jr. and the Champion. The Juiceman Jr. is marketed by Trillium (800 800-8455) and can be purchased from Sears for $90. I used Champion juicers for 6 years before receiving a Juiceman Jr. for Christmas. It takes a little more time to clean up than the Champion, but seems to extract more juice with less pulp and less temperature build up. I have used it daily for over a year and it has held up well.

Champion juicers are made by Plastiket (209 369-2154) and are known to last a long time. I have had two wear out after about two years of heavy usage. In both cases the seal wore out, which costs about $55 plus shipping for Plastiket to repair. I've also noted that the screen clogs up over time and should be replaced about once a year (under $4). Despite these drawbacks, I view my Champion juicer as the smartest $160 I've ever invested. They make great tasting juice, and can be assembled and cleaned quickly.

If a juicer heats up substantially when being used, it can reduce the nutrient/enzyme quality of the juice. The Champion does pretty good here except with stringy vegetables such as celery and parsley. This problem can be solved by slicing them into chunks before juicing.

Surprisingly, both the Juiceman Jr. and Champion do a reasonable job with wheat grass, which is one of the most important juices to consume.

Systematizing the Juicing Process

→ The following are the techniques I use to minimize the number of steps and decisions I have to make each time I juice, thus reducing the time and effort required:

- I leave my juicer on the counter at all times. A portion of my kitchen counter space is designated as my "juicing area". This is right next to my sink.

- I set aside shelf space right above the juicer as the "drying area". When done juicing, I place the rinsed components on a paper towel for them to dry. This saves me from having to dry them by hand.

- I use the same bowl (to catch the juice) and holding dish (to set the washed produced on before juicing) all week. They are just rinsed off after each use. I have a designated place for each of these. The holding dish goes right behind the sink so the water actually drains into the sink. The rinsing bowl is placed on the edge of the sink but could just as easily be placed in the "drying area" cupboard with the other juicing parts.

- I have designated certain areas in my refrigerator for juicing supplies to minimize the amount of time I spend looking for things.

- When using the Champion juicer, I used plastic produce bags to catch the pulp, and a wire twist to hold the bag in place. With the Juiceman Jr., I put plastic bags in the pulp bucket so it doesn't have to be cleaned.

Refrigerator Layout
Carrots, melons, misc.
Salad materials
Fruit
Primary juicing supplies Celery, spinach, cukes, peppers, cabbage, etc.

Lemons, avocados	Beets, potatoes

- I organize my shopping list as follows: juicing basics and rotationals. The items listed in Figure 6.1 are the juicing basics I try to juice each week (you could add "organic if available and affordable" after every item except the carrots, which I insist be organic). Items juiced periodically include: red cabbage, cantaloupe, watermelon, honeydew, brussel sprouts, romaine lettuce. See the references at end of this chapter for more complete suggestions.

Food	Quantity
Organic carrots	5-10 pounds
Apples	5 pounds
Parsley	1 bunch
Celery	1 bunch
Garlic	½ of a bulb
Ginger	2 inches of root
Beets	1 (golf ball size)
Green bell peppers (I don't juice the seeds)	2 - 5
Kale	1 bundle
Wheat grass	1 small 4"x4" tray
Spinach	1 bundle

4) ONCE OR TWICE A DAY CONSISTENTLY

My objective is to juice once or twice a day on a consistent basis. Consistency is more important than "bingeing out" periodically. When working long hours, I sometimes purchase fresh juices by Odwalla. These are a day or three old, taste great, and are the next best thing to juice made on the spot. Odwalla is expanding their distribution network, so keep your eyes peeled for their refrigerators in your stores near the produce department.

5) CARROT/APPLE BASE

I use a 75% base of organic carrot/apple juice and then add the intense vegetables (beets, kale, spinach, etc.) around that. Note:

- Apple is the only fruit that can be combined with vegetable juice.
- Dark green juice is too concentrated to be taken straight and is thus hard on the liver if consumed without dilution.
- Dark green juice usually tastes bad by itself (in my opinion). The carrot/apple base makes consuming the other vegetable juices more palatable.
- Organic carrot juice is the single most important juice you can drink.
- I don't juice apple seeds, just in case there's some truth to the rumors that they contain small amounts of strychnine. This issue isn't addressed in any juicing book I've read.
- Tart apples are best, as recommended by healing pioneer Dr. Max Gerson. I prefer Granny Smith.

Since you will be drinking a fair amount of carrot juice, it is essential that you locate a reliable source of organic carrots. Carrot is the only ingredient that I insist be organic. When I've tried juicing non-organic carrots in the past, I seem to gradually lose interest in juicing.

When the price of organic carrots goes up over 80 cents per pound, I cut down on the quantity and try to substitute apples, cucumbers, or celery. I still have a hard time paying over a dollar a pound for organic apples so I usually purchase non-organic apples.

How much to drink per session depends on your individual circumstances. What sounds good to you? When I started, I drank over 25 ounces per session. For the last couple years, about 16 ounces (12 ounces carrot/apple and 4 ounces greens) has "felt" about right.

6) EMPHASIZE VEGETABLE JUICES

If I only have time to juice once or twice a day on a regular basis, I want to get the most bang for my nutritional buck, so I drink primarily vegetable juices. In general, vegetables contain more nutrients than fruit. I like to eat fruit far more than I like to eat vegetables. Thirdly, common sense tells me it is far easier for my body to extract nutrients from fruit than woody, fibrous vegetables. It would probably take me an hour to eat the plate of vegetables that I juice and drink in ten minutes every morning.

There are times when I make exceptions to this rule. Some mornings, the carrot/apple/greens juice just doesn't "sound good" to me. Other mornings, the prospect of a fresh fruit drink sounds just too good to pass up. Cantaloupe, honeydew and watermelon are the highest nutrient content fruits. Most of the nutrients are in the rind which is inedible. When the rind is juiced along with the rest of the melon, the result is a taste I really enjoy. I usually cut away any part of the rind that looks weird, especially with cantaloupe. When in doubt, cut it off and throw it away. I use organic melons whenever possible for juicing. Juicing non-organic melons seems no different than juicing non-organic apples, I just wash them as thoroughly as possible and always use a scrub brush on cantaloupe. There are pesticide removal sprays available for the extra cautious.

In the wintertime, when melons are not available, I occasionally drink freshly made orange or pineapple juice, which tastes nothing like what you get in the cans and bottles. Apple lemonade is another favorite substitute (3-4 apples plus 1/4 or 1/2 a lemon WITH the rind). **Do not juice orange peels!** You can juice pineapple rind. However, I usually throw most of it away because my understanding is that tropical fruits often come from places where pesticide usage laws are less stringent. Plus, all those nooks and crannies makes it very difficult to wash thoroughly.

I usually give my body one day a week where I do not drink vegetable juices. On this day I emphasize fruit juices, rest, and minimal amounts of food in general. This frees up nerve energy for cleansing and gives my digestive organs a rest. **You are not what you eat, you are what your body is able to assimilate.**

7) *VARIETY IS KEY, SO VARY THE REMAINING 25%*

Scientists have labeled certain types of nutrients with letters: A, B, C, D, E, K, etc. Yet plants know nothing of our vitamin coding system, and the nutrients that plants concoct are based on formulas provided by mother nature. The nutrients are balanced to form a synergistic whole, and the components and proportions may not be fully understood or classified. Rather than wait for scientists to catch up with mother nature, I like to go right to the source: plants. Since different plants emphasize different elements, I try to vary that remaining 25% (what I add to the 75% carrot/apple base) as much as possible throughout each week, month and year. The idea is to provide my body with access to as many of the trace elements it needs to fully nourish my cells, thus relieving my organs of the burden of having to generate the missing nutrients internally. In truth, it is probably not possible to fully achieve this, but the basic approach I use seems to have a good chance of providing a sufficient base of material to generate that which is lacking.

I complement the nutrient variety this strategy provides, with supplements that are 100% pure food grown. One source of food-based supplements is the Living Source Food-Grown Nutrient Systems made by Rainbow Light Nutritional Systems. Their address is 207 McPherson Street, Santa Cruz, CA 95060. I take one of their Superfood supplements occasionally along with my morning juice. Each Superfood tablet costs about 20 cents and contains the following nutrients:

Spirulina (500mg), Chlorella (100mg), Bee Pollen (100mg), Wheat Grass (100mg), Barley Grass (100mg), Beet [root], 12mg, Spinach [leaf], 12mg, Carrot [root], 12mg, Red Pepper [fruit], 12mg, Celery [herb], 12mg, Parsley [herb], 12mg, Lemon [peel], 12mg, Jujube [fruit], 45mg, Siberian Ginseng [root], 33mg, Schisandra [fruit], 33mg, Rehmannia [prepared root], 25mg, Atractylodes [root], 16mg, Fu Ling, 16mg, Dong Quai [root], 16mg, Lovage [root], 16mg, Cinnamon [bark], 16mg, Astragalus [root], 16mg, Morinda [root], 11mg, Fennel [seed], 11mg, Lycium [fruit], 11mg, Shiitake [fruiting body], 11mg, Nettle [tops], 11mg, Licorice [root], 11mg.

These Superfood pills are a shotgun approach to filling in the trace mineral gaps in my nutrient intake. I may be wrong, but my "taste buds" seem to agree here—these Superfood pills actually taste okay. However, I never take any supplements when I've included wheat grass in my juice. My taste buds give me a very strong "NO" signal in this matter. This may be due to the fact that wheat grass is so nutrient dense.

8) USE ORGANIC PRODUCE WHENEVER POSSIBLE

Organic produce is higher in nutrient content and usually tastes better than non-organic. It is grown without the use of pesticides and should therefore contain virtually no chemical residue.

A side benefit from buying organic is that you help support farmers who are attempting to be more gentle on the environment. A primary reason that the American Bald

Eagle was placed on the endangered species list was the impact DDT build up was having on their reproductive efforts. Massive use of pesticides is playing crapshot with nature. We really don't know what the cumulative effects will be. We have the technology to grow organic and should support the farmers going the extra mile to apply it.

For many years, organic produce gained a reputation as "not looking too good" (i.e., usually covered with spots, smaller than the non-organic produce, and somewhat shriveled up). I have been buying organic produce now for over 6 years and can tell you that if the organic produce looks like this in your store, you need to find another store. The organic produce I buy looks better and healthier than non-organic! I don't mind paying up to 25% more for organic produce given all of these factors.

Transitional Produce

To qualify as organic, fields in which produce is grown must go at least 2 years without the use of pesticides. Produce grown on the fields during this 2 year period is referred to as transitional. It's not technically organic even though no pesticides are used. I want to support the farmers making the transition, so I buy this produce whenever I can fit it within my budget.

Pesticides/Chemicals

While I try to buy as much organic produce as possible, I do not let the possibility that the non-organic produce may contain pesticides deter me from juicing once or twice per day. Unless the bag of potato chips, box, bag or can of food you buy says "made from organically grown..." on it, chances are pretty good it has an equal amount of pesticides.

Here's the scale of produce in preferred order:

1. Grow as much of your own produce as you have the time/inclination for. A great book on this is: *How to Grow More Vegetables Than You Ever Thought Possible on Less Land Than You Can Imagine*, by John Jeavons. Published by Ten Speed Press.

2. Buy organically grown or transitional.
3. Buy locally grown produce.
4. Buy produce marked as "pesticide residue free". Fred Meyer's produce section has pioneered an effort to do this, at least here in Washington State.
5. Buy from a produce department supplied by a conscientious produce buyer - one who shops for nutrient quality. Remember, you vote with your dollars. If you accept less, that's what farmers will produce.

Where to buy Organic Produce

The best organic produce I have found is grown by Cal-Organic Farms (805-845-3758), which apparently is also the largest organic produce farm in the United States. To locate their produce in your area, I would first call the local health food stores listed in the "Health Food Products—Retail" section of your phone book yellow pages.

9) DRINK IMMEDIATELY AFTER JUICING

I drink juice immediately after making it. Fruits and vegetables are alive! When juiced, the nutrients and life force start to dissipate. In some cases, such as cabbage, this occurs quite rapidly. According to a study quoted by Jay Kordach in his juicing tapes, 80% of the vitamin C is gone within 1 minute! The nutrients in green cabbage known to help heal stomach ulcers also dissipate extremely fast.

The second reason to drink juice immediately is enzymes, as discussed earlier in this chapter. They are the life force in the food. You have heard it said that cooking food destroys vitamins. You must also realize that heating any juice over 120 degrees Fahrenheit kills enzymes. According to Jay Kordach, this forces the pancreas to work overtime generating the enzymes necessary to digest the food.

10) JUICE ON AN EMPTY STOMACH

Your objective is to get the nutrients into your bloodstream as quickly as possible so they can nourish your trillions of cells. To get into the bloodstream, the nutrients must first pass through the stomach, into the intestines, and finally through the intestinal villa. This process seems to be facilitated by drinking the juices on an empty stomach. My energy level seems higher if the juices are taken on an empty stomach.

This is also consistent with the principle of nutritional hygiene: *Don't drink liquids with your meals as it tends to dilute the digestive fluids and thus slow the process of digestion and assimilation of your meals.* Slowing digestion and assimilation consumes more energy. Nutritional value may be compromised if food spoils in the stomach. For more information on this read *Fit For Life* by Harvey and Marilyn Diamond. (*Fit for Life* has sold over four million copies making it the best selling diet-health book ever according to the Diamonds.) Better yet, experiment for yourself. Try eating the same meal two days in a row. Drink liquids with one meal and skip them the next—see if you notice a difference.

As mentioned earlier, over the years I've developed the habit of nibbling on the carrots and apples while preparing the juice. My body seems to be telling me to do this.

11) FEED YOUR MIND WHILE YOU JUICE.

I keep a cassette tape player near my juicing area so I can listen to educational tapes which feed my mind with fresh ideas at the same time I am feeding my body. Audiotapes can be listened to while you are doing other things. Thus, it is easier to listen multiple times than to read a book multiple times. Reading requires your full attention. Given that reviewing helps the compound learning process, audiotapes allow you to retain a higher percentage of the material covered. Additionally, this added educational benefit helps make it personally ecological to juice consistently.

Here are some suggestions on where to find educational audio cassette material:

- Educational cassettes can be checked out from your local library. Electronic search tools may allow you to search by medium.
- Nightengale-Conant (800 323-3938) carries the most comprehensive catalog of educational/self-development audiotapes that I am aware of.
- Audio-Tech Business Book Summaries (800 776-1910). For $135, this service will send you 34 audio book reviews of top business books over the course of a year. Each review is 30 minutes in length and begins with a 5 minute synopsis of the key ideas presented in the book.
- Books on Tape (800 626-3333) makes a good case for having the world's largest selection of unabridged audio books including over 2,500 best sellers. This is a great source for biographies in addition to carrying several self-development titles.
- Some bookstores and video stores. The more people that ask for them, the more they will supply.

VARIOUS JUICING ISSUES

Here are a few more points I'd like to make that didn't get covered in the above discussion:

"DON'T I NEED THE FIBER?"

Fiber is essential for maintaining a healthy digestive system. The juicing strategy I'm suggesting is primarily designed to supplement your existing meals.

IRRADIATED FOOD CAUTION

Irradiation is a technique used to prolong shelf life of "fresh produce" by exposing it to certain types of radiation. The thought of this doesn't exactly thrill me. Common sense tells me to avoid food that has been irradiated.

"BUT I ENJOY EATING"

Let me ask you a question. If you drink soda pop, does that prevent you from eating your meals? Just think of juicing as creating your own can of soda pop. However, rather than "shooting blanks" at your six trillion cells, you are loading your body up with powerful nutrients it needs to cleanse and build a strong healthy body at the same time you are quenching your thirst. A side benefit to juicing for some is that by providing their body with more of the nutrients it needs, the less "hunger pangs" it sends off, and thus the less they have to eat during and between meals.

"I DON'T HAVE TIME FOR JUICING"

There is a time management principle called Quadrant II described by Stephen Covey in his book, *The 7 Habits of Highly Effective People.* Covey suggests concentrating your efforts on <u>important</u> tasks before they become <u>urgent</u>, thereby gaining maximum leverage from your time investments. Juicing is Quadrant II time at its best. I believe it is far easier to keep myself healthy than it would be to cure myself once ill. Juicing helps keep me healthy by nourishing my trillions of cells with the finest nutrients nature has to offer. Juicing is not something that is urgent, but it is most definitely important.

Also note that knowledge work is intangible. Subtle shifts in energy levels and mental clarity can literally make the difference between something taking hours to complete vs. just few minutes. When creating a software application, hundreds of decisions must be made each day. One wrong decision can lead me down a path that costs hours. Juicing supports my efforts to operate in a peak state a high percentage of the time.

THE PESTICIDE ISSUE

Non-organic produce contains pesticides and should therefore be washed thoroughly if organic produce is not available. There are vegetable washes available which can help remove pesticides. I don't use them in the interest of time, which may turn out to be a mistake. As stated earlier, I use organic whenever possible, especially carrots, which covers the majority of the produce I'm consuming. The remaining produce is washed thoroughly, but I don't use vegetable washes (to simplify the process). Food in cans and bottles is no less immune to pesticides than fresh produce. You do have to be careful of anything you consume in large quantities.

ECOLOGY

If you are concerned about consuming excessive resources by juicing, try to compensate by cutting back in other areas. According to John Robbins, author of the landmark book, *Diet for a New America*, you can save more water by not eating one hamburger than you can save by not showering for six months.

COMPOST YOUR PULP IF POSSIBLE

Since most of the nutrients have been removed from the juice, I don't recommend using the pulp for baking or salads. The best use seems to be to place it in a compost pile and thus recycle the material into the soil. The carrot pulp tastes a great deal like sawdust.

NIBBLING AND CHEWING YOUR JUICE

I nibble on the produce while preparing the juice. While this is probably not recommended by the "experts", I do it because I enjoy the taste of the food and it gets my digestive system revved up. If you don't nibble, then you should "chew your juice"—at least the first couple drinks, by sloshing them around in your mouth. One doctor encouraged me to mix a little of the pulp back in with the juice to prevent my blood sugar level from rising too fast. I discussed this issue with a representative from Robbins Research International who seemed extremely knowledgeable. He believed that the sugars in fresh produce are different from sugar in candy, and the body converts them into blood sugar at a slower rate.

JUICING SUMMARY

Since everyone is unique, juicing may benefit some more than others. I am absolutely convinced that juicing has significantly enriched the quality of my daily life. If you are new to juicing, I hope the above guidelines prove useful as you take the leap of faith required to experiment. If you have already tried juicing, I hope this discussion will renew your enthusiasm that juicing can be practical for time conscious knowledge workers.

If you want to give juicing a try, the smartest money would be to order a copy of the Juiceman audiotape series from Trillium at (800 800-8455). Note that they sometimes make special offers on juicers that include these cassettes. There is something about the way Jay Kordach presents ideas about juicing that inspires people to do it. These tapes contain very important information for couples planning to have children.

OTHER MENTAL CLARITY DISTINCTIONS

OPTIMIZING NUTRIENT INTAKE

Juicing is a great source of nutrients, but it doesn't eliminate the need or desire to eat. Here are a few topics in the area of optimizing nutrient intake that have proven helpful. Most of these are covered more thoroughly in the book *Fit for Life* by Harvey and Marilyn Diamond and Chapter 11 of Anthony Robbins' book, *Unlimited Power*.

FOOD COMBINING

Some foods should not be eaten with others. Proteins are digested by acid based fluids while starchy carbohydrates are digested by alkaline based fluids. If you eat meat and potatoes at the same meal, it will take much longer to digest because the digestive fluids will neutralize each other. This causes foods to remain in the stomach much longer, spoil, and requires much more digestive energy to process. Robbins' book mentioned above includes a food combining chart with specific guidelines. You can begin to follow this rule by eating only one concentrated food (i.e., not a vegetable) at each meal, and by eating it with a salad or lightly steamed vegetables.

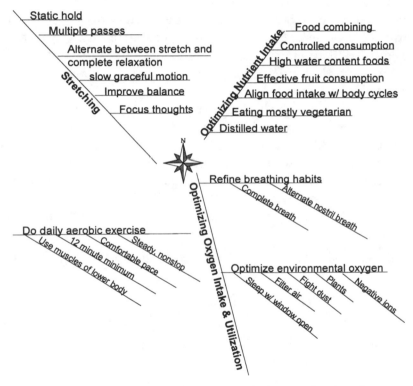

Figure 6.1. Mindmap of other mental clarity distinctions.

"The ability to transform energy and even create it within you is one of the profound secrets of life. Like a tree, you are one of the great power-stations of nature."

— Master Lam Kam Chuen

Controlled Consumption

Eating a huge meal will wipe out the benefits received from every other guideline in this chapter. To quote the Diamonds, "Even the finest, most nutritious food available will spoil in your system if it is overeaten." Robbins' teaches that the best way to eat a lot is to eat a little. "That way, you'll be around long enough to eat a lot."

"You cannot be a man of action if you overeat and under-exercise."

— Napoleon Hill

Uncooked High-Water Content Foods

How long have we been told that cooking destroys vitamins and minerals? In practice, I apply this understanding by eating or juicing uncooked fruits and vegetables as much as possible. These are high-water content foods which are relatively easy to digest. However, I also consider cooked organic brown rice and pasta to be healthy meals. We need variety in our meals, so I'm extremely disciplined with about 80% of my foods, and allow whatever flexibility feels appropriate for the remaining 20%.

Effective Fruit Consumption

Anyone who thinks fruit gives them intestinal gas should try eating that fruit on an empty stomach. If you do this, and only eat one type of fruit at a time, it will quickly move into the intestines and be digested in under 15 minutes. If the stomach isn't empty, the fruit gets held up in the stomach, and that's where the gas comes in. Fruit eaten on an empty stomach is one of the healthiest things you can do for your body. Fruits energize and cleanse.

Timing of Food Intake to Align With Body Cycles

The idea here is that our bodies are designed to cleanse themselves from about 4 am to 12 noon, to eat from noon to 8 pm, and to assimilate food between 8 pm and 4 am There is much conflicting literature on the importance of eating breakfast. I use the "most of the time" rule on this one as well. Most of the time, my breakfast is fruit (orange, grapefruit, or melon when in season) which is followed about 15 minutes later with a carrot/apple/veggie juice. If I get hungry before noon, I usually eat fruit or make more juice.

Not eating anything at least 2 hours before bedtime has always made sense, but I must confess that this is a rule I've had difficulty following at times. If this is an issue for you, consider trying VATA TEA from Maharishi Ayur-Ved, available at health food stores or by calling (800 255-8332). This herbal tea contains just natural ingredients: licorice, ginger, cardamom and cinnamon. It's like drinking a candy bar and has a calming effect on the digestive system.

EATING MOSTLY VEGETARIAN

What do the following people have in common: George Bernard Shaw, Benjamin Franklin, Thomas Edison, Ghandhi, Albert Einstein, Leonardo da Vinci, Voltaire, Sir Isaac Newton, Henry David Thoreau, Dr. Albert Schweitzer, Aristotle, Tolstoy, Pythagoras, Plato and Socrates? According to Anthony Robbins, they were all vegetarians. Coincidence?

In a speech at the University of Washington, John Robbins, author of *Diet for a New America*, eloquently stated the case for eating vegan: "I'm so happy that it fits together—that the food choices and life choices that are most freeing for me; that are best for my health and best for yours; that give us bodies that are the most open vehicles for our spirits; that function the best; that live the longest; that have the least disease; that have the strongest resistance in our immune systems; that are least prone to degenerative diseases—those same choices are the kindest; cause the least suffering to other animals; cause the least drain on the resource base of our culture and our world; are most ecologically sustainable; allow the rain forests to be rain forests, to be habitats for all those wild animals and plants and indigenous cultures."

In September 1992, Paul Harvey News reported the following results from research conducted by Elder George Vandeman in Thousand Oaks, California:

- Middle age males who regularly eat meat suffer from fatal coronary disease three times more often than vegetarian men of the same age.
- A meat-based diet has been linked to a disproportionate incidence of breast and colon cancer, high cholesterol, high blood pressure, angina pectoris, osteoporosis, kidney stones, urinary stones, and rheumatoid arthritis.

According to Paul Harvey, several related studies have demonstrated that such health problems can be reversed with a vegetarian diet.

Dave Scott—six time winner of the grueling Ironman Triathlon—has been a vegetarian for the last 15 years. Apparently he gets his protein from vegetarian meals which include soy and the soy derivative, tofu. Cindy New of Montreal, winner of this year's Montreal Marathon, has been a vegetarian for the last 12 years. She was quoted as saying that most world-class runners experimenting with high-energy foods have become vegetarians. She believes that nuts, grains and vegetables "provide all of the protein necessary for good health and vigor."

There have been times when I've gone for months without eating meat of any kind. To be fair, I must mention that I'm now in a mode where I eat meat very selectively (usually fish) once or twice a week. Why? The primary reason is that I've been working over 70 hours per week between programming and finishing this book. Due to this time crunch, I've been relying on the cafeteria at work, and this limits my selection. The other reason is that I'm still experimenting. While each of us is different in our nutritional needs, one thing seems pretty clear: our society has been conditioned to consume far more meat than we need.

DISTILLED WATER

Most people have caught on to the fact that our tap water quality has deteriorated over the years. I've been using distilled water as recommended by Anthony Robbins and the Diamonds, and find it agreeable. Distilled water tastes so neutral that I can drink it at room temperature without adding any flavorings.

OPTIMIZING OXYGEN INTAKE AND UTILIZATION

Oxygen is the most important nutrient we consume. We can go for months without food, days without water, but only minutes without oxygen!

In their "Mentally Tough" audiotape, Dr. James Loehr and Peter McLaughlin describe the strategy Bobby Fischer used to defeat Boris Spassky for the 1972 chess title. Fischer hired a physiology specialist to study videotapes of Spassky's matches to determine why his performance declined towards the end of long matches. The specialist concluded that it was due to the slumped posture Spassky used throughout the match. This posture diminished the oxygen flow to his brain, which eventually got the best of him. As a result, Fischer altered his training to boost oxygen flow to his brain. He started swimming underwater for as long as possible in order to build lung capacity, and this, among other things, helped him win.

The brain consumes over 20% of the oxygen we take in, even though it makes up only 3% of our total body weight. Given that oxygen is one of the brain's primary fuels, it makes sense to consider ways of optimizing the flow of this nutrient to the brain. Three main strategies for acting on this distinction are:

- Refine your breathing habits
- Optimize environmental oxygen
- Do daily aerobic exercise

REFINE YOUR BREATHING HABITS

Your breathing pattern can significantly influence your energy level. The increase can be so profound, that yoga teachers recommend mastering asanas (stretches to discipline the body) before doing pranayamas (breathing exercises). If you don't have the discipline to direct the increased energy levels resulting from pranayamas, it can be harmful.

→ Not all breaths are created equal. It is often helpful to walk outside in the fresh, non-processed, non-dried out air and take a few complete breaths. A complete breath involves the following steps (note that all breathing should be through the nose for these exercises):

1) Empty your lungs by exhaling completely. Contract the abdomen as necessary. Be intelligent. Pay attention to any signals from your body that you may be overdoing it. There should be no straining during any part of this breathing exercise.

2) As soon as you've completely exhaled, begin to fill your lower lungs with air by expanding the abdomen. You're doing it right if your stomach sticks out and your chest doesn't move.

3) When your lower lungs are filled with air, then begin filling the upper lungs by expanding the chest area.

4) When you think you have inhaled as much as you can, try raising the shoulders a bit and see if you can inhale a little more.

5) Hold this breath for five to ten seconds or until your body tells you it would be wise to begin exhaling.

6) Completely exhale and repeat these steps.

Both inhaling and exhaling should be done in a controlled manner. "Don't let the air just come gushing out," to quote Mr. Hittleman. According to Harvey and Marilyn Diamond in *Fit for Life II*, we should emphasize abdominal breathing, since the lower part of the lungs absorbs 80% of the oxygen.

This next exercise sounded weird to me when I first heard of it. However, when I finally got around to trying it, I found it to be useful. I try to remember that usefulness overrides weirdness in many cases. Alternate nostril breathing quiets the mind. I find this especially useful after getting all pumped up to deliver a speech or presentation at a meeting. "By understanding that each nostril connects to the opposite side of the brain and using this information in a breathing exercise, you can actually balance the two sides of the brain, and the result is an amazing sense of equilibrium," according to the Diamonds. The steps are as follows:

1) Block one nostril with your thumb and the other with your ring finger. Your index and middle finger go on your forehead.
2) Breath in through the right nostril, hold for five to ten seconds, then block the right nostril and exhale through the left.
3) Inhale through the left nostril, hold for five to ten seconds, then block the left nostril and exhale through the right.

The Diamonds recommend repeating this six times to achieve the desired effect. When doing this, they recommend that you hold your breath for about half as long as it takes you to inhale or exhale.

One of the quickest ways to quiet your mind and increase your ability to concentrate is to change the way you are breathing.

OPTIMIZE ENVIRONMENTAL OXYGEN

→   Here are a few suggestions for optimizing the quality of oxygen in your environment:

- Sleep with the window open, at least where it is safe to do so.
- Try an Allergy Free air filter as recommended by Paul Harvey (800-ALLERGY).

- Give your home an occasional air bath as Ben Franklin used to do. This involves leaving all windows and doors wide open for a few minutes, especially when it is very windy out.
- Fight dust in every way you can.
- Keep plants in your environment, especially in an office where the air is highly processed.
- Soak up negative ions by spending time in the outdoors as often as possible, especially in the mountains or near water.

DAILY AEROBIC EXERCISE

"Exercise is the greatest medicine ever invented."

— *Covert Bailey*

➔   I greatly admire the contribution Covert Bailey has made to the field of exercise and health. He teaches what I consider to be the most important principle of weight control: you can improve your body's ability to burn fat with consistent aerobic exercise. The number of calories you burn when you exercise is not as important as exercising in a way that changes your cell metabolism.

The way to improve your cell metabolism is to exercise aerobically 4-6 times per week, for 12-30 minutes each workout. Bailey teaches that you need to get your heart rate up to certain levels and keep it there for the duration of the workout. An important point is that you should be able to carry on a normal conversation while doing this exercise. Otherwise you are working too hard.

The heart is a muscle as well, but we cannot exercise it directly. It gets exercised when we mobilize the large muscles in the body and thus force the heart to pump more blood to them.

"We exercise to change muscle chemistry so that we will burn fat more efficiently."

— *Covert Bailey*

Aerobic exercise in summary:

- Is steady, nonstop.
- Lasts a minimum of 12 minutes.
- Has a comfortable pace.
- Uses the muscles of the lower body.

For many knowledge workers, the key question is how to fit exercise into a busy schedule. One way is to systematize—to develop what I call exercise engrams. You know you have an exercise engram when you only have to make one decision to perform the exercise. Virtually everything else is done on automatic pilot. I have a gym bag in my car at all times and have committed my weight workout to memory. All I have to do is get to the gym and my body pretty much takes over from there. I know exactly how long it will take, and am careful to avoid distractions so my workouts won't interfere with other responsibilities.

To develop an engram, you set time limits and obey them strictly. Design a workout that makes sense for you and then commit all the steps to memory. You can organize yourself to minimize the number of decisions that must be made once you've decided to work out. In truth, decisions will have to be made, but you will have defined the context so clearly, that making them takes very little effort.

If going to the gym isn't an option, consider purchasing a minitrampoline for $30 at a Target store. I'm on about my sixth one, and have found the Dunlop brand to be the best made for the money. The book *Fit for Life II* offers suggestions on minitramp workout techniques. I just alternate between jumping jacks and running in place with my arms over my head, my objective being to use as many muscles as possible in the workout.

Another excellent aerobic exercise machine is the Health Rider ($500), designed and marketed by Covert Bailey. My Mom has had good luck with a similar but less expensive ($200) machine called a Cardio Fit which is available at Fred Meyer and Kmart stores.

STRETCHING

➜ In addition to encouraging people to eat the right foods, the inventor Dr. NakaMats emphasizes participating in the "right athletics". He does not feel that jogging, tennis and golf are conducive to generating creative brain waves. You may get ideas while doing these things, but NakaMats feels they probably won't be your best ideas. I get my best ideas when I'm doing exercises that require a lot of discipline. For me, this means stretching. This section gives you an overview of material available for refining your stretching habits.

> *"Getting old is not a matter of age; it's a lack of movement."*
>
> *— Anthony Robbins*

The best book I've found on stretching is called *Stretching* by Bob Anderson. In it, Anderson explains the rules for stretching, what stretches to avoid, and gives specific routines for each sport.

Another excellent source of stretching information are books and tapes by Callan Pinckney. Her "Callanetics" routines are a synthesis of exercises she learned while traveling around the world. She teaches the "Pelvic Curl" and other exercises which emphasize strengthening muscles that support a healthy posture, but which aren't exercised in most workouts. Among other things, I like her concept of doing things in "triple slow motion".

The stretching information with the most impact I've ever found has been an introductory yoga video by Richard Hittleman. Little did I know when I rented that $3 video from Blockbusters that it would have such a profound positive impact on my life. He shattered my preconceptions about yoga being something for "hippies" only. I was surprised to learn, from other sources, that Kareem Abdul-Jabbar credits yoga with allowing him to play as long as he did without injury. Supermodel Kim Alexis, on a recent Larry King show, strongly endorsed yoga. She mentioned that Jane Fonda now does yoga more than any other exercise. Yoga is recommended by the Diamonds in *Fit for Life II*, by recent books by Harvard Professor Andrew Weil, and by healing pioneer, Dean Ornish.

Yoga has three main components: stretches (asanas), breathing exercises (pranayamas), and some philosophical underpinnings. You do not need to understand the philosophies in order to benefit from the stretching and breathing exercises. There are as many levels in yoga as there are in the game of tennis. Just because you're not ready for Wimbledon doesn't mean that you can't participate and enjoy the benefits from the activity. If you would like to begin by attending a class, I encourage you to attend one based on the teachings of B.K.S. Iyengar. The following Internet url is the home page of one of the top yoga trainers in the country, Aadil Palkhivala. If you can't attend one of his classes, his staff may be able to point you in the right direction.

```
http://www.yogacenters.com/yoga/
```

➜   Skeptical beginners may want to start with Richard Hittleman's books and videos which can be ordered from the following address:

Clear Lake Productions
P.O. Box 3007
Santa Cruz, CA 95063
The following summary of stretching guidelines was synthesized from all of the above sources:

• Use a static hold. Do not bounce. You want to move to a position of moderate stretch and then hold it without movement. Avoid straining or forcing. Breath in a relaxed manner while holding the position.

- Use a multiple pass approach. Hittleman has you do each stretch three times, and rest momentarily between each attempt. This allows the body to work its way up to a more complete stretch in a less stressful manner.
- Alternate between stretch and "complete relaxation". After each stretching exercise, you are encouraged to "relax completely, without movement" for a few moments. This allows the body to equalize itself after energy flow has been increased by the release of tension.
- Use a slow graceful controlled motion. This is the part that requires a lot of discipline for me. Since my normal energy usage pattern is to do things as quickly and efficiently as possible, "slow and graceful" is "synergistic oscillation".
- Balance. Several of the stretches in yoga are designed to improve your balance and to balance the sides.
- Think about the area being stretched. You might even try visualizing the area being stretched as surrounded by blue or white light. Imagine the color going out with your breath when you exhale. If you do it right, the tension gets washed away as the color is exhaled.

Some stretches require caution. For example, I've injured my neck twice doing the plow. Both injuries occurred as a result of not being adequately warmed up, and I may have been doing it improperly as well. I'd also wait a while before trying a headstand. Here are a few guidelines for stretching:

- Stretch before meals or 90 minutes afterwards.
- Do it in a place where you have plenty of fresh air.
- Do it in a quiet place where there will be minimal distractions.
- Use a towel or mat.
- Dress in comfortable clothing.

According to Richard Hittleman, the spine must have continual and methodical exercise. In his book, *Be Young With Yoga*, Mr. Hittleman writes that a unless it receives the proper care, the spine gradually becomes compressed, stiff, and actually constricts. This causes a person to become even less active, which stiffens the spine even more. Hittleman believes that this vicious circle can be broken when a person begins to manipulate their spine through the careful practice of yoga. He believes this is true regardless of age.

CONCLUSION

A key distinction many people overlook is that healthy eating, breathing, stretching and regular exercise are not just about extending your life span or reducing your lifetime medical bills (although they probably do these things as well). The key benefit to these activities is the improvement in the quality of every moment you are alive. Adopting these habits can improve the quality of life you experience at each moment, whether that moment involves knowledge work or sharing yourself with family and friends.

Vince Lombardi stated that "Fear makes cowards of us all." Similarly, an infusion of personal energy can inspire us to set our sights on more challenging horizons. While capacity can be increased by acquiring specialized knowledge and skill, this won't do you much good if you don't have the energy to apply it. The more energy you cultivate, the more discipline it takes to direct that energy into productive channels. You must also maintain a balance between cycles of exertion and cycles of recovery, which leads us to the issue of personal ecology.

CHAPTER 9

PERSONAL ECOLOGY

Simplifying my life has been one of the most complicated things I've ever attempted.

— *Anonymous*

You can become the fastest reader, the most creative genius, build teams of extremely bright people for conducting synergistic dialog, become a fast learner, establish highly organized information management systems, develop high levels of personal energy, and take on projects that give you an opportunity to employ huge levels of untapped intellectual resources; but if you consistently violate the rules of personal ecology, you risk wiping out all the gains you achieved in these other areas.

Each life is maintained by a complex series of relationships. When something happens in one area that throws the overall system out of balance, a series of forces are mobilized to correct the situation. I use the term personal ecology to describe the ongoing process of keeping your life in balance. When engaging in an activity which threatens this balance, I say that it is not "personally ecological". Personal ecology is governed mostly by subconscious mental processes designed to help keep you alive. If you do something which is not personally ecological, these subconscious mental processes usually figure out some way to distract you from doing that activity.

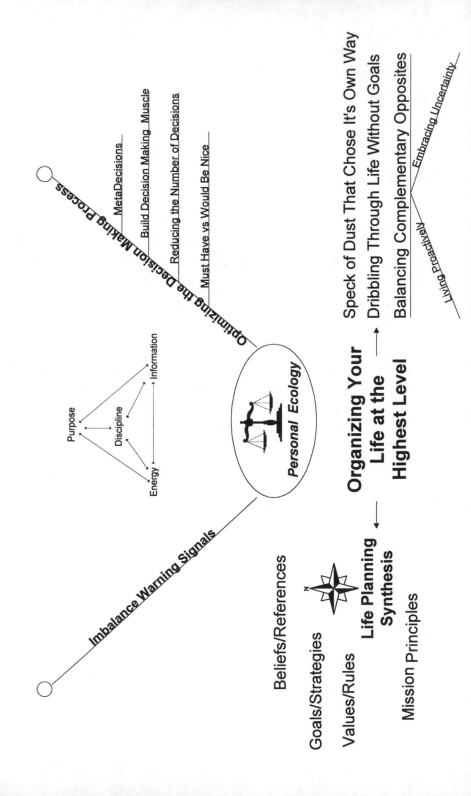

Optimizing the Decision Making Process

MetaDecisions

Build Decision Making Muscle

Reducing the Number of Decisions

Must Have vs Would Be Nice

Speck of Dust That Chose It's Own Way

Dribbling Through Life Without Goals

Balancing Complementary Opposites

Embracing Uncertainty

Living Proactively

Imbalance Warning Signals

Purpose

Information

Discipline

Energy

Personal Ecology

Organizing Your
Life at the
Highest Level

Life Planning
Synthesis

Beliefs/References

Goals/Strategies

Values/Rules

Mission Principles

For example, it takes discipline to have a strong work ethic. It also takes discipline to balance this mental activity with adequate emphasis on the other dimensions of life: physical, spiritual and social/emotional. If your work ethic is not disciplined, and consequently these other dimensions are neglected, eventually the subconscious mental processes responsible for maintaining personal ecology will figure out a way to divert you from work. For myself, this often meant getting sick, which forced me to stop working, at least until I figured out how to eat and exercise in a way that diminished my susceptibility to flu viruses. Eventually my back started bothering me from long hours of sitting, or I'd do something stupid which would throw my back out and make it almost impossible to sit in front of a computer. By not disciplining my work ethic, I was throwing myself out of balance and bringing into play a series of forces that eventually diminished my ability to work.

While in my twenties, I owned a plant that looked something like Figure 9.1. One day it dawned on me that the more this plant grew, the more likely it was to fall over from its own weight. In many ways, the same was true for me.

During this time I was single, spent very little time with family and friends, was running my own business without any employees due to inadequate financing, and went for years

Figure 9.1

without taking a week off. My work week often ended at 12 midnight on Saturday evening, since Sunday was my day off. My idea of a healthy meal was natural peanut butter and strawberry jam on the cheapest brown bread ($.33/loaf) I could find, and was usually eaten while I continued working or while driving. I was not attending church regularly and did not connect regularly with my support network.

Now, such a pace might work for a week or two—for example, when coming down the home stretch on a major project—but as a predominant way of life for several years, I was asking for trouble. These tendencies eventually caught up with me, and I made some bad decisions which forced lifestyle changes. The above ideas are presented so you will understand that it was a combination of things that contributed to the imbalance.

When Esther Dyson said, "People who succeed in the computer industry tend to accumulate more and more power until they implode," this was something I could relate to. The more I succeeded as a computer consultant, the greater the demands that circumstances and other people placed on my time. Eventually, the weaknesses in my life management systems were exposed, and I crashed and burned. I could relate to Forrest Gump when he ran clear out of the stadium after scoring a touchdown: he didn't know when to stop either.

PRINCIPLES

My mission with *Brain Dancing* is to help you mobilize untapped intellectual resources within the context of a balanced lifestyle. At this point I'd like to define what I mean by balanced lifestyle.

> A balanced lifestyle is one where you are happy most of the time, adhering to healthy habits, and managing your time for optimum effectiveness.

In John F. Kennedy's words, "Happiness is the full use of your power along lines of excellence."

➔   There is an abundance of information available that you can use to improve your life. How fast can you climb and still maintain balance? That depends on your ability to direct your energy into applying information towards a specific purpose in a consistent and disciplined manner. This last sentence is summarized in Figure 9.2.

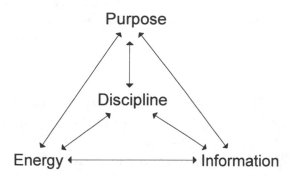

Figure 9.2

The fundamental truths that govern our lives are not written in English nor any other natural language. Any attempt to describe them in their entirety is analogous to the parable of the six blind men and the elephant. Each man touched the elephant in a different place, and each came away with a different impression of what an elephant looked like. When it comes to fundamental truths, we are not unlike these blind men. Each person "touches" the fundamental truth elephant in a different way depending upon the context they have defined for their lives. The above diagram doesn't apply to everyone nor every situation. However, it is useful in understanding the idea of personal ecology as I have described it throughout this book.

This diagram was inspired by Peter Senge's systems theory as discussed in *The Fifth Discipline*. Systems theory addresses the relationships between elements in a system. Leverage is attained by identifying the limiting factor that if changed, would have a favorable impact on the overall system. Discipline is the leverage point in self-development. You will have as much energy, and be aware of as much information, as you can apply towards a worthwhile purpose in a disciplined manner.

Your capacity is enhanced when there is an increase in any one of the above dimensions. Personal ecology is at risk any time you expand your purpose, energy or information awareness without a corresponding increase in discipline. The following discussion elaborates on the interplay between these four elements of personal capacity. It is my attempt to answer the following questions:

?   Why do many people die soon after retirement?

?   Why do many people fear public speaking to such a degree?

?   Why do people often procrastinate reading a book when they know it would be highly applicable to their current situation?

?   Why do teachers seem to come into our lives when we are ready for the guidance they have to offer?

ENERGY RIVER THEORY

→   Have you ever wondered why people often die soon after retirement? The project-oriented nature of my career has given me the opportunity to experience several "mini-retirements". The problem that arises for me is what to do with all of the energy I was directing towards the project. It feels analogous to having a river blocked so that the water backs up and spills out into other areas not accustomed to the excess energy. This process of redirecting large amounts of energy has been fairly stressful at times. It may be the anticipation of this energy redirection that makes some projects so difficult to complete.

Hans Selye touched on this when he wrote, "I think we have to begin by clearly realizing that work is a biological necessity. Just as our muscles become flabby and degenerate if not used, so our brain slips into chaos and confusion unless we constantly use it for some work that seems worthwhile to us."

Public speaking is another situation requiring the disciplined use of energy. Isn't it amazing that people often fear public speaking even more than death? One of the reasons for this is that standing up before an audience often results in a massive surge in energy. This is due in part to having lots of people focusing their attention on you. You can label this extra energy fear or excitement, but the bottom line is that you must learn to direct this energy in healthy ways or public speaking may actually be life-threatening. One of the simplest ways to do this is to free up your hands so that you can gesture freely and expressively. Use that energy to move your body energetically.

In an earlier chapter I mentioned Anthony Robbins' skill as a public speaker. He speaks with more energy than anyone I've ever seen. On more than one occasion, I've noticed that he was actually drenched with sweat an hour or two after beginning to speak. By using public speaking energy on stage with intensity and power, he almost turns it into an athletic event.

In Chapter 4, I mentioned that visually-oriented people talk faster, and that this allows for higher bandwidth conversations. Anybody can develop the ability, or flexibility, to switch into visual mode for such a conversation. However, such conversations may be harmful to individuals who have difficulty turning off the adrenaline flow after the conversation. For some people, discipline is the price for making fast paced conversation "ecological" for them. Others seem adept at such conversations without using adrenaline energy. It takes very little effort for them to go at a rapid pace.

As mentioned in Chapter 8, yoga students are encouraged to master *asanas* (body postures and stretches) before they begin refining their skills with *pranayamas* (breathing exercises). Asanas help you manage existing energy flows in the body, whereas pranayamas cause an increase the flow of energy. Yoga teachers warn that violating this principle can result in significant damage to your brain and nervous system. This energy redirection aspect of yoga can make it difficult at times. It is also a primary reason why yoga has been one of the most valuable disciplines I've ever pursued.

Chapter 5 pointed out that when doing right brain mode activities, it is easy to lose track of time. Setting time limits and adhering to them is the discipline that opens the doors to mobilizing right brain mental processes. I also pointed out that it takes an act of discipline to override this tendency to habitually prefer one mode (right or left brain). This is because doing this often requires you to establish a new "energy river" in your mind. The process is similar to walking along a trail in a forest. At some point you notice that the trail doesn't lead directly to where you want to go, so you veer off the trail and plow through tall grass and brush to get there. The first time down this trail is the toughest, but gradually you wear a new path and it gets easier with each journey. This is how you form a new habit of thought—a new energy river.

Personally, I'm in a constant battle with discipline when it comes to eating. This may be due to the fact that I've worked long hours for several years and could use about a month off to fully regain my balance. During this time, I've been directing as much of my personal energy through my mental batteries as possible. Writing this book hasn't been the most relaxing diversion from brain intensive work at Microsoft. One of the ways I give myself a break is by eating. This redirects energy into my stomach and gives my brain a break.

On mornings when I'm feeling particularly weary from the long hours and weekends, it is tempting to swing by the cafeteria for a mind numbing bagel, or plate of hash browns loaded with ketchup. But, as often as possible, I resist the temptation and settle for an Odwalla fresh vegetable juice. My experience has proven time and again the truth of Emerson's words when he wrote in *Compensation*, "...we gain the strength of the temptation we resist." When such a temptation is resisted, it strengthens that muscle within that allows us to redirect energy into activities we deem important, in spite of the direction of current emotional winds.

Ending a sexually active relationship is difficult for the same reason: you must redirect or diminish the flow of sexual energy. One reason it is wise to wait until marriage is because this is so difficult to do. Napoleon Hill describes a related theory in his "Sex Transmutation" chapter of *Think and Grow Rich*: "So strong and impelling is the desire for sexual contact that men freely run the risk of life and reputation to indulge it. When harnessed, and redirected along other lines, this motivating force maintains all of its attributes of keenness of imagination, courage, etc., which may be used as powerful creative forces in literature, art, or in any other profession or calling..."

Teenagers not involved in sports are at a disadvantage in that they must find other disciplined ways to use the increased energy associated with that phase of life.

We must become disciplined energy processors. Even if your goals are written out to the *nth* degree, and you do everything you've learned to increase your energy level, all is for naught if you don't have the discipline required to direct that energy towards achieving your goals with consistent action and disciplined thinking. Jim Rohn was right on the mark when he said, "For every disciplined effort, there are multiple rewards." This is true because it increases your fundamental capacity for effective action.

DISCIPLINED INFORMATION USE

Information shapes our lives in countless ways, as does a lack of information. As mentioned in Chapter 1, we are in fact, in-formation. We learn that a new food lowers cholesterol, so we eat more of it. We learn that a certain type of exercise reduces risk of heart disease, so we do more of that, etc.

What about the book that sits on your desk? The one you know you should read to help you get over some current stumbling blocks? The one you somehow never get around to reading? With the information comes a responsibility to use it wisely. Doing this requires discipline to direct energy into new pathways, and some people would rather go through life with ignorance as their scapegoat.

The truth is, you may not be ready for that information. There may be a situation in your life that demands more of your attention. It may be that the information in the book, if applied, would change your life in more ways than you are ready for. It may increase your capacity in ways that you may not be ready to handle. As the amount of information we are aware of expands, so does the number of choices we can make. Sometimes, we may not yet have the strength of character required to make such new choices wisely. The section on "decision making" later in this chapter addresses this notion further.

Developing your visualization muscle is a powerful mental skill. The information presented in Chapter 3 on how to develop visualization skills should only be applied to the extent that you can use this new capacity in a disciplined manner. Thinking in pictures allows you to think both positive and negative thoughts more efficiently. Therefore, you must simultaneously develop the discipline required to maintain control of your thoughts.

For example, if someone begins discussing negative situations in your presence, you must turn off your visualization skills momentarily to prevent the corresponding images from appearing in your mind. Thoughts are things; they are first cause. If a person is avoiding the development of this skill, I believe it is due in large part to them not being ready to exercise the mental discipline which would make it ecological for them to proceed. Personally, my skills in this area have been increasing steadily for several years, as opposed to all at once.

PURPOSE

As the amount of information we are aware of expands, there is an increasing need to clarify our objectives so as to narrow the band of relevant information. We then must exercise the discipline to direct most of our attention towards information relevant to that outcome. It often amazes me how many "interesting" distractions pop up as I attempt to narrow my focus. *Useful* information must come before *interesting*.

Clarifying or enriching our sense of purpose can also open doors to new information. Continuing the book avoidance example above, if you decide that you are ready for advancing your personal development, then ask yourself what context would make it necessary for you to read and apply the ideas in the book. It may be that you only need to look at your current situation from a different angle (see the discussion of metaphors in Chapter 3 for related ideas). In other cases you may need to create a new context, or a new purpose altogether.

One way to enrich context is through visualization. Truly effective visualization generates creative tension. It takes discipline to direct this tension, or energy, into the actions that will make your dream a reality. Sometimes it takes discipline to not act until you are ready. "Creative tension" is the term Peter Senge uses to describe what goes on in a person's mind when they acknowledge the gap between the way things are now and the way they would like them to be.

Shopping provides us with a microcosm of the creative tension experience. Consider a situation where you are shopping and see something that you really want but can't quite afford. You could buy it right then and there by putting it on a credit card, so you definitely believe it is a reality that can be manifested. However, if you don't act on the impulse to buy immediately, then to the extent that you care about owning that item, you will experience creative tension. As the energy of creative tension begins to flow in the core of your being, ideas will present themselves to you as to how this tension can be released. Creative tension will begin to present alternatives to your awareness like cutting back a little here, working a few extra hours there, taking on additional projects, selling something, or you name it.

Some of these options may be quite tempting, especially as you continue to hold on to the awareness of the gap between current reality and how things could be. To the extent that you can allow creative tension to run its course until the right moment (with no compromise of basic principles), you have increased your capacity for effective action by the disciplined use of purpose.

Chapter 3 referred to Alan Kay's statement that, "It's not what the vision is, it's what the vision does." Effective visualization generates creative tension: a force driving you towards new levels of creativity and action. Discipline comes in when you have to decide whether or not to act. Ask yourself if you can truly afford the time, energy and money this choice will require, or if you need to wait until you're better prepared. Ask yourself if this alternative is consistent with your values (i.e., the boundary conditions you've established up front).

> *"If you have a lot of energy, and don't know what you want, you're what we call 'dangerous'... You're like fuel spilled all over the place, and wherever someone drops a match, kaBoom!, that's where you go."*[14]
>
> *— Anthony Robbins*

Creative tension results from both a candid acknowledgment of where you are and a belief that you are capable of manifesting the vision. Shopping for your dreams *as if* you are ready to decide is one way to step into the future and create the required feeling of certainty. The lesson for knowledge workers is this: do whatever it takes to step into the future and experience your goal as if it is about to come true. Use that experience to solidify your belief that it will come true. Then step back and allow the energy of creative tension to flow through your life and work its wonders.

---

[14] From Anthony Robbins' Personal Power video, *The Keys to Your Unlimited Success.*

DISCIPLINE

The above discussion explained the interplay between the four fundamental aspects of personal capacity: energy, purpose, information and discipline. Rarely do we make a change in one of these dimensions without a corresponding change occurring in the other areas. As you exercise the discipline to develop your ability to direct energy into productive channels, you are increasing your capacity for managing success. This discipline develops the character that supports the process of making sound decisions, and thus makes it more likely that you can maintain balance as you begin to succeed. In many cases, this discipline involves making sound judgments in the face of expanding options due to your success.

"Almost everyone can handle adversity. But, to test a persons true character, give him power."[15]

— Abraham Lincoln

OPTIMIZING THE DECISION-MAKING PROCESS

I began Chapter 1 by stating that decisions represent the fulcrum of mental effectiveness. In the spirit of "going meta", this section discusses ways of optimizing the decision-making process.

As mentioned in Chapter 6, Richard Bandler believes that some people get by with lousy decision-making skills because they aren't motivated to do much. By making sure his clients have an effective decision-making strategy before teaching them a powerful new motivation strategy, Bandler increases the chances that they will use the increased motivation wisely.

What are the elements of a good decision-making strategy? Effective decision making is an art, and having a great strategy is no guarantee that it will be applied intelligently. We make hundreds if not thousands of decisions each day at

---

[15] As quoted in *Beyond Success*, by Brian Biro.

various levels of consciousness. To apply a conscious process to every decision would quickly overwhelm us with what Alvin Toffler called "decision stress".

→   The decision-making process should begin with one or more metadecisions which classify the relative importance of decisions and identify which elements of your decision-making strategy should be applied. J. Edward Russo and Paul Schoemaker use the term "metadecision" to describe choices about the decision process itself—choices that are likely to determine the character of the whole effort. Several of the following metadecisions were adapted from their book, *Decision Traps: The Ten Barriers to Brilliant Decision-Making and How to Overcome Them*:

?   What is the central issue involved? Is there a larger issue "upstream" that is driving the need for this decision?

?   What type of decision making process should be used to make this type of decision? How long do decisions of this nature usually take? How much energy and resources are typically required?

?   To what degree does this decision affect other decisions?

?   Must this decision be made at all? Now? By me, or should others be involved?

?   When should the decision be made? Are the deadlines arbitrary?

?   Can this decision be made by proceeding sequentially through the decision making process, or will it require a more iterative approach?

?   Where should I concentrate my time, energy and attention? How much time should I expect to spend on each phase of the decision process? Do I face a difficult job framing this choice?

?   Can I draw on feedback from similar decisions in the past to improve the quality of this decision?

? What skills, biases and limitations do I have that may impact my ability to deal with this issue?

? How would a more experienced decision-maker whom I respect handle this issue?

? How will I handle pressure to decide quickly so often encouraged by those who stand to benefit from such behavior? Salespeople often do this by instilling a fear of "missing out" in buyers.

? What steps can I take to minimize or avoid buyer's remorse?

After addressing issues raised during the metadecision process, effective decision making involves the following steps to varying degrees:

- Clarify the decision to be made. What is the central issue being decided and why? Examine the chain of events that led to the need for this decision. Russo and Schoemaker recommend that you invest time optimizing the frame of mind in which the decision will be made. They write, "The way people frame a problem greatly influences the solution they will ultimately choose."

- Establish boundary conditions for evaluating options. How will you know that you made a good decision? What factors must be present for you to proceed?

- Generate options and evaluate. Gather intelligence. Whenever possible, base decisions on facts rather than hunches.

- Identify and access risks. Those with high downside risks require more time and energy.

- Perform an ecology check. Under what conditions would you not want to carry out this decision? Whom and what else could it effect?

- Learn from feedback.

Chapter 6 described a layered reading strategy that helps you become highly selective in the material you read at

→ slower speeds. As discussed in Chapter 1, Peter Drucker writes that effective executives reduce the number of decisions required of them by focusing their energies on strategic decisions at "the highest level of conceptual understanding". These high level decisions then provide a framework within which other people can make decisions more easily. Effective executives I've had the chance to study aggressively pursue the information that will help them make important decisions. Better information means better decisions, and the fewer decisions they have to make, the more energy they can invest in making them well. This also applies to knowledge workers desiring to manage their time more effectively. The next section of this chapter on organizing your life at the highest level is a direct application of this idea.

Another key technique for minimizing the number of decisions you have to make is to use habits and engrams. "Time teaches all things to he who lives forever but I have not the luxury of eternity," writes Og Mandino in his classic, *The Greatest Salesman in the World*. The first law he teaches is to "form good habits and become their slaves".

→ In his breakthrough book, *Psycho-Cybernetics*, Maxwell Maltz observes that it takes about 21 days to form a habit. He also points out that the ultimate habit, the "meta habit", which tends to influence the formation of all the rest, is that of our self-image. For a complete discussion of effective habit formation, you are also encouraged to read Benjamin Franklin's autobiography and Stephen Covey's book, *The 7 Habits of Highly Effective People*. Each time I refer back to Franklin's thirteen virtues, I seem to understand them better and increase my appreciation of the staggering wisdom upon which they are based.

As the number of choices in our lives increases, there is an increasing need for structure, for habits, for making decisions that last. Chapter 8 described how I use juicing and exercise engrams to reduce the number of decisions I need to perform these activities. When I juice or exercise, I pretty much just make one decision—to begin—and my body takes over from there. Granted, I started out by carefully designing and continually refining both of these activities. The key benefit is that by reducing the number of decisions involved, I've removed a barrier to doing them. It is the same process we use to learn to drive. Use it to reduce the number of decisions required to carry out frequently performed tasks.

Napoleon Hill observed that, "People who succeed make decisions quickly and change minds slowly if ever." The clearer you are about your goals and values, the easier it is to recognize an opportunity consistent with them, and to quickly reject all others. When anticipating an important decision, I've found it helpful to create a one page summary that separates essential criteria from the "would be nice" issues. For example, when shopping for a house, I created a sheet that listed my top five criteria as follows:

Must Have	Bad ← Rating → Excellent				
1. Quiet neighborhood	1	2	3	4	5
2. Convenient location	1	2	3	4	5
etc.	1	2	3	4	5

This was followed by additional criteria that I would consider pluses, but didn't consider essential.

Would be nice	Bad ← Rating → Excellent				
1. Hot tub	1	2	3	4	5
2. All appliances included	1	2	3	4	5
etc.	1	2	3	4	5

When a potential house showed up on my radar screen, this sheet allowed me to quickly reject a great many houses that otherwise would have eaten up my time. When a strong candidate showed up, I could more easily afford to thoroughly research the decision.

Decision making is a skill developed by making decisions. Work your way up to big decisions. In his *Personal Power* audio tape series, Anthony Robbins emphasizes that our decision-making muscles must be strengthened daily by making decisions and following through with action.

In some cases, you may want to use Ben Franklin's technique. He took a blank sheet of paper and drew a line down the middle. After writing the pros on one side and the cons on the other, he crossed them off as they balanced each other out. For example, a single pro item might offset two or three cons.

With this perspective on the decision-making process, I will now discuss the ultimate form of "going meta"—organizing your life at the highest level. This involves making a series of decisions about how you will run your life. For myself, learning how to work hard has been the easy part. Learning how to organize myself so as to perform that work within the context of a balanced lifestyle has been a different story. To quote Ross Perot: "The principles of management and leadership are simple. The hard part is doing them, living up to them day after day, not making lots of excuses for ourselves. You know all those complex management theories? They're just an excuse for not facing up to how hard it is to live by some very basic principles."

ORGANIZING YOUR LIFE AT THE HIGHEST LEVEL

Have you ever noticed how life sometimes wraps up valuable lessons in the simplest of moments? This happened to me once back in college when all I did was sit down in my car seat. Up came this cloud of dust, and the sun shining through my windshield made sure that I noticed. I brushed it away with my right hand, and most of the dust went to the left. I noticed one spec however, that started to the left, and then veered up and to the right.

Upon closer examination, I could see that this was not dust at all but rather a tiny little bug. Perhaps because this bug was so small, it made me stop and wonder what was in this speck that made it so different from all the rest.

Life!

This little speck contained the stuff of life, and was thus blessed with the ability to choose its own path, regardless of which way the wind was blowing.

I once asked Norman Cousins, author of *Anatomy of an Illness*, if there was any one event in his life that got him started on the path of such amazing accomplishments. "Yes, as a matter of fact there was," he responded. After a pause that seemed like minutes, he continued, "I was born!"

Each of us has been blessed with the miracle of life, and thus the ability to choose our own path, regardless of which way the wind happens to be blowing in our life at any given moment.

There are three basic strategies for running your life: going with the flow (totally right brain), schedule everything you do and do everything you schedule (left brain), or some combination of both. Chapter 5 encouraged you to use the synergy of opposites to enhance creativity, and I believe we can also find synergy in the opposites of willpower and going with the flow. Sometimes there is wisdom in the wind!

Not long after "imploding" from overwork and underplay, I was dribbling the ball at a soccer clinic one Saturday afternoon. Two defenders stood between me and the goal, and I was working hard to get by them. Suddenly the clinic director blew her whistle and declared: "OK, now we're going to play without goals."

The goal markers were removed and play resumed. I just stood there. One minute I was working aggressively to dribble past the defenders towards the goal, and the next, I didn't know which way to go. The defenders resumed their attack, and I dribbled away from them. Now we were playing "keepaway".

Reflecting on this event afterwards, the lesson was clear: I was dribbling through life without goals! Rather than working proactively to create a life I had chosen, to a large extent, I was simply reacting to whatever challenges life tossed my way.

You may be wondering where the synergy of opposites lies. Yes, this experience encouraged me to exercise willpower by directing my life proactively. However, I did not plan on learning this lesson that afternoon! Learning a life lesson was not on the schedule. I was just there to play soccer. In *The Celestine Prophecy*, James Redfield does a masterful job of explaining how to embrace such coincidences.

Deepak Chopra, in his book, *The Seven Spiritual Laws of Success*, addresses the issue of balancing the laws of intent and desire with the laws of least effort and detachment. With these laws, Chopra presents these seemingly opposite notions: "Inherent in every intention and desire is the mechanics for its fulfillment." And, "In detachment lies the wisdom of uncertainty...in the wisdom of uncertainty lies the freedom from our past, from the known, which is the prison of past conditioning. And in our willingness to step into the unknown, the field of all possibilities, we surrender ourselves to the creative mind that orchestrates the dance of the universe."

Balancing the application of these two opposites is where the tire meets the road in self-development. The rest of this chapter focuses on the willpower side of the equation.

→   One of the excuses I had frequently used to avoid an intensive goal setting session was that I wanted to be in an absolute peak state of mind and body. I viewed goal setting more as an event than an ongoing process, so I wanted to be darned sure that I wrote down the "right" things.

Well, this "dribbling through life without goals" metaphor really lit a fire under me. I reasoned that if all I did was wait for the next gust of wind to blow before using my ability to choose my own way, then the wind would still be in control! So I set a date and began exercising and eating as healthy as I knew how.

My goal setting day finally arrived and after four hours of brow knitting thought-intensive writing, I had several pages of goals. The excitement from having accomplished this soon clashed with reality when Monday morning arrived, and all of the urgencies of my ongoing responsibilities kicked in. I felt a lot like the steamship captain mentioned in Chapter 2, who must look far in the distance to chart his course, because he knows that his ship will continue in the same direction, long after he has turned the wheel.

Gradually (and with Stephen Covey's help), life has taught me that developing a personal mission statement and goals is more of an ongoing process than something you can wrap up in a single day. "These are things you have to 'detect' more than invent," in Covey's words.

The next time the winds of circumstance begin to blow in your life, remember that little speck of dust that chose its own way, and then get on with the *process* of 'detecting' your way. The following material demonstrates how to apply the three-step mindmapping process presented in Chapter 5 to help you accomplish this. The better the tools, the better the end result is likely to be.

LIFE PLANNING SYNTHESIS FOLDER

> *"When we talk about time management, it seems ridiculous to worry about speed before direction, about saving minutes when we may be wasting years."[16]*

> — *Stephen Covey*

→   Organizing your life at the highest level is the ultimate form of "going meta". The life planning synthesis folder is a simple manila folder containing the following five sections:

- **Mission Statement:** The special contribution you would like to make—how you want to be remembered. To quote Peter Senge, "...first and foremost the bedrock

---

[16] For a complimentary four-week sample of the Seven Habits Organizer, call 1-800-680-6839. This is an excellent introduction to Covey's time management principles.

of what draws us into action is that we deeply care."
What is it that you truly want to create in your life—
what do you deeply care about? Listen to the song,
"Climb Every Mountain", from *The Sound of Music*. You
know you have found your mission when you have
found a dream you can give all the love you can give
every day you're alive. Find a dream that "juices" you—
a dream towards which you can apply the very essence
of who you are.

- **Principles:** This section is a one page mindmap of the
  fundamental true north principles that govern our lives.
  This is something you evolve through time to reflect
  your best understanding to date of what these
  principles are. When you learn a great idea, this sheet
  will allow you to evaluate its importance as it relates to
  other valuable lessons you've learned. Figure 9.3 is an
  example of this type of mindmap. Remember the
  fundamental truth elephant—create your own from
  scratch based on your own perspective on fundamental
  principles.

- **Values and Rules:** What is most important to you,
  expressed in terms of the states you would like to
  experience daily, and those you would like to avoid.
  Next to each value, place the rules you use to determine
  the extent to which you are living these values. A
  primary benefit of clarifying values is to optimize your
  decision-making process. Values are often the
  fundamental criteria used to accept or reject an option.
  Refer to *Awaken the Giant Within* by Anthony Robbins
  for details on this topic.

- **Goals/Strategies:** What are your top goals in each of
  the four main areas of life (physical, mental, spiritual,
  and emotional/social)? Work-related goals are expressed
  in terms of the skills you would like to develop and
  problems you would like to be able to solve (i.e.,
  capacities). Evidence procedures for recognizing when a

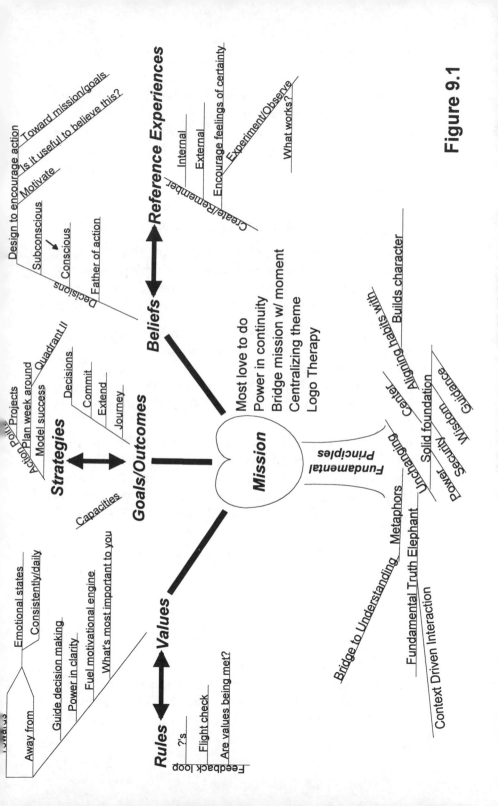

Figure 9.1

goal is achieved and symbolic representations of key strategies are included here.

- **Beliefs/References:** What beliefs will you need to support the achievement of these goals? When you realize that your beliefs are a choice, the next logical step is to select beliefs in alignment with your mission, values, etc. What reference experiences do you have (or need to create) to support these beliefs at a gut level?

I try to keep the number of pages in this folder to a minimum. Each of these sections is developed using an extended version of the three-step mindmapping process discussed in Chapter 5. The process goes something like this:

- Get five unlined sheets of 11"x17" paper and start an idea collection sheet for each of the above categories. By "start" I mean just write the purpose of the sheet (example: "Mission") in the middle of the page. I seem to have better luck with these if I turn the sheets sideways.

- Place these sheets in a 9"x12" manila file folder and label it "Life Planning Synthesis". Don't fold these large sheets until you absolutely have to. I find that having the crease in the middle of the page disrupts the flow of ideas. I only fold them after I have placed a substantial number of ideas on the page.

- Periodically schedule 30-minute sessions to brainstorm one or more of these topics. The 30 minutes are divided up something like this:
    - Set a timer for 5 or 10 minutes and write as many ideas on the sheet as quickly as you can.
    - Take a five minute break to minitramp, go for a quick walk or stretch out.
    - Spend the remaining 15-20 minutes adding any additional ideas to the sheet that come to mind. During this time, feel free to consult reference

texts such as those by Anthony Robbins or Stephen Covey.

- Set the sheets aside for a day or two. In the mean time, place a stack of Post-it notes in your purse, wallet, or your time management system if you carry it with you. Anytime over the next few days that an idea comes to you regarding one of these sheets, write it on one of these notes. If your time management system has room, you can also write these ideas there.

- The next time one of your 30-minute life planning sessions rolls around, these notes can be reviewed during the second half of the brainstorming process. Add the useful ideas to the appropriate idea collection sheet.

- Repeat the above process until you feel like you have accumulated a critical mass of ideas about each section. Now it's not so intimidating to plan that 4-hour session because you are ready for it!

- Plan a day when you will have about 4 hours of uninterrupted time. If possible, go to a hotel near the ocean or other body of water. Prepare yourself for this day by taking especially good care of your health. Make a special effort to exercise and eat as healthy food as possible.

- When the day arrives, use a similar process of oscillating between intense brainstorming and right brain stimulating breaks. The desired outcome from this event is either highly organized mindmaps or written statements for things like your mission statement or strategies. Use symbols and reference favorite metaphors as much as possible. Being able to traverse the various ideas as rapidly as possible helps you view each individual idea within the context of others.

This folder is a tool for centralizing all high level life-management documents. Before doing this, I had goal sheets stored in several places. This was a result of doing exercises in books and at seminars. If someone asked what my goals were, I had to stop and think which ones I should refer to. The folder system also gives you a convenient reference tool when doing your weekly planning.

> *"You know I thought I had mono once for an entire year—turned out I was just really bored."*
>
> — *From the movie, Waynes World*

This exercise also allowed me to align multiple activities synergistically. It's not unusual for a single activity to contribute simultaneously to 2 or 3 key goals. For example, each time I gave a speech at Toastmasters club, I used it as an opportunity to refine the material in this book. Everything in this book also applies to the process of writing, giving speeches and developing computer software. As I applied this material to speaking and my work, I was able to further refine my understanding of what ideas were truly useful, and thus should be included in this book. I learned to synthesize, synchronize and synergize. That is: synthesize life management ideas into a coherent set of documents, and use the perspective this folder provides to synchronize as many activities as possible for maximum synergy.

How do you know if you did a great job on these documents? To paraphrase the words of Alan Kay, it's not what the documents are, it's what they do for you. Neat and pretty is irrelevant unless what you end up with is a set of ideas that consistently inspire you to action.

> *"First you have to have fun. Second, you have to put your love where your labor is. Third, you have to go in the opposite direction to everyone else."*
>
> — *Anita Roddick*

➔ For many years I was careful to avoid participating in multi-level marketing companies. Then along came Fund America. This company had made deals with major companies such as Citibank and MCI, and was being endorsed by several people I had great respect for. I pulled out my electronic spreadsheet to analyze the opportunity, and my excitement went through the roof! All of a sudden I was launched. I was leaping out of bed in the morning, bounding with newly found energy, and getting more excited about this opportunity all the time. After careful thought, I decided that it would distract me from my main area of focus. As much as it hurt, I let this one go.

But what a lesson this experience taught me! Where did all of this energy and excitement come from? It came from within. It was there all along waiting to be tapped by the right combination of circumstances. I believe this same level of energy and excitement exists within each individual, and that you aren't done with your life synthesis folder until those sheets of paper unleash these resources. Two quotations from Anthony Robbins sums this up well: "People aren't lazy, they just have impotent goals," and, "Giant goals produce giant motivation."

What was unique about the Fund America opportunity that made such an impact? I could clearly relate to the substantial benefits, and I believed it was possible for me to achieve them. Emotionally, I had stepped into the future and felt the gap between where I could be and where I was. I had discovered "creative tension".

So how do you translate the above words into the true experience of creative tension? Seeing is believing. Do something as if you are ready to realize one of your dreams. Visualizing your dream helps, but you can help out your visualization efforts with a variety of activities. You can go shopping, interview someone who has already done what you want to do, or visit a company or department that has done something similar. These activities can substantially boost your visualization efforts by providing the raw material (sights, sounds and emotions) for more effective visualization. Getting to know someone who has already done something dramatically impacts my belief systems about what is possible for me. Since everyone is different, other strategies may work better for you. Seek until you find.

The subconscious is the seat of action. Ultimately, the purpose of this work is to communicate a concise message to your subconscious in a way that ignites your action-oriented engines. The effectiveness of any communication is not what is said, but rather the meaning that is effectively transferred. Sometimes patience is in order.

Golden Gaval winner Peter Legge tells a story of Chinese bambo that lies underground as an undeveloped plant for four years. In the fifth year it finally emerges from the soil and grows a foot the first day. From then on, with all these years of nurturing behind it, it adds a foot a day until it reaches a height of about 100 feet.

> *"People often overestimate what they can do in a year, and underestimate what they can do in a decade."*
>
> — *Anthony Robbins*

Sometimes when you set a goal, to truly achieve it, you must shore up the framing and solidify the foundation.

You can use things in your environment: sights, sounds, smells, temperatures, seasons, etc., to remind you of key components of your life planning synthesis. I often use symbols of the powerful forces in nature (Mt. Rainier, crashing waves, the stars at night, etc.) to remind me of what nature is capable of. Since I'm a part of nature, I must have access to at least some of these resources, at least to the extent that I am able to direct them towards a worthwhile cause.

BRIDGING THE MISSION WITH THE MOMENT

➔   I've found it helpful to associate daily activities to my highest values and mission statement. My Toastmasters club had a visitor one day promoting leadership by participating in community activities. She talked about her work with the Campfire Girls organization and why it inspired her to participate. She had linked up in her mind that she was touching the future of our country by making this special effort to nurture our future leaders. Given the passion with which she spoke about this topic, these were not just fancy sounding words, they were words she lived and breathed every moment she participated in that organization.

I can give you two examples of how I apply this strategy in writing this book. On April 27, 1994, I read an article about someone donating twelve million dollars to the federal government to help pay off the national debt. The article pointed out what a trivial impact this donation would have since the debt, as of April 24 totaled $4,558,348,698,138.33. It reminded me of a television show I'd seen where Japanese bond traders decided to emphasize the contribution they were making to our bond market. One day they boycotted the U.S. market, and it went to its knees. American traders were just wandering around with nothing to do until about one in the afternoon, when the Japanese decided they had made their point. In my mind, the lesson was that we have actually compromised our fundamental freedom as a nation by running up such a huge debt. I care deeply about my country. I keep an American flag next to my desk to remind me that the toughest day at the office pales in comparison to the average day on the front line. Given what I knew about the link between capacity and desire, I could see that such a financial burden will absolutely shape the destiny of our nation.

If giving twelve million dollars to the government won't help, then I wondered what an individual could do to make a difference in this situation. My answer was to try to mobilize untapped intellectual resources of America's knowledge workers. If it is true that most people are using less than 10% of their mental capacity, then if I could figure out a way to unleash even an additional 10% of a large number of people over an extended time period, this might compound and actually have an impact. I concluded that this was our nations greatest underutilized resource!

> *"Within each of us lies the chance for greatness in some area. Identify that gift which is unique to you, and in your pursuit of developing that gift, let no one deter you in your task."*
>
> *— from the movie, Chariots of Fire*

If this wasn't enough to inspire me to write, I learned from a Paul Harvey news broadcast that the comet Tuttle was expected to pass fairly close to our planet in the summer of 1994. There was some speculation that this comet could actually strike Earth on its next pass in the year 2130. This inspired me to write a speech entitled "The Dance of Life", describing that day in the future when all nations on Earth pool their resources to create and launch a rocket to blast this comet out of the sky before it slammed into our planet. Birds have the gift of wings, horses the gift of great running speed, and flowers great beauty. Only humans are blessed with the gift of intellect capable of saving "team Earth" from this catastrophe.

If such a day should arrive, would it come down to the abilities of few engineers working several all-nighters with lightening fast reading speeds and amazing creative skills? Probably not. Our chances seem much better if a significant number of people begin using even 10% more of their intellectual capacity on a consistent basis over the decades preceding this event. The benefits from this activity would compound to increase the capacity of our planet, and give our scientists and engineers a fighting chance.

These may seem like crazy ideas, but that's all they are— ideas. The important thing to note is that they did inspire me to invest hundreds of hours into this book. Their value stemmed from their emotional impact. What ideas will it take to inspire you to act on your dreams?

SYSTEMS THINKING

→   Peter Senge's book, *The Fifth Discipline,* is an excellent overview of the vast and rich set of distinctions referred to as "Systems Thinking". He writes that when some people rise above the trees and see the forest, all they see is a bunch of trees. Senge's ideas have profoundly impacted every chapter in this book. This entire chapter is an application of Systems Thinking to the overall process of mobilizing untapped intellectual resources. The idea is to see through complexity in order to identify the underlying structures generating change. This involves identifying the balancing processes built into the system that are currently limiting growth. If these balancing processes are not identified, working harder may just cause these balancing processes to kick in more. When applied in the context of personal ecology, make sure you understand the benefit you are receiving from such limiting factors before reducing their influence in your life. The best example I can think of is the way some people sabotage their financial success because they are not ready for decisions resulting from the increased flexibility.

Senge explains that there will always be more limiting processes as you grow. As each source of limitation is overcome, growth returns until you bump into a new source of limitation. These words can hardly do justice to the ideas Senge conveys in *The Fifth Discipline.* I recommend the "Limits to Growth" exercise in Chapter 6 of Senge's book.

BURNOUT WARNING SIGNALS

→   If you ever find yourself out of balance, remember that it is probably due to a combination of factors, and will probably require a combination of changes to return to balance. How do you know when you are out of balance? If there are problems in your life, it may mean that the universe is trying to get your attention. To quote Shakti Gawain, "If you don't pay attention, the problems will intensify, until you finally get the message and start to listen more carefully to your inner guidance."

Here are some other indicators that I watch out for:

- The quality of my relationships with others is a great measure of emotional stability. People often serve as mirrors. Every person is in my life for a reason.
- If I'm having trouble making eye contact with others.
- If I am having trouble forgiving someone. To quote Joseph Murphy, "If I should tell you something wonderful about someone who has wronged you, cheated you, or defrauded you, and you sizzle at hearing the good news about this person, the roots of hatred would still be in your subconscious mind, playing havoc with you." It's usually easier to deal with such situations when I haven't depleted my life energies with overwork for extended periods.
- Tendency to notice mistakes others are making, which upon closer examination, are really projections of mistakes I'm making.
- Actions inconsistent with feelings.
- Having difficulty being honest with myself or identifying true feelings, making it somewhat challenging to be honest with others. A good test for this one is to go for a long drive and notice if any ideas seem to nag at my consciousness.
- If I'm not dealing with time pressures well. If I'm rushing around with high levels of anxiety, not concentrating on being fully present each moment.
- Having difficulty saying "no" to unexpected demands on my time.
- Noticing that I haven't been laughing much lately.
- Having difficult concentrating, often getting distracted by random worries.
- Frequent bingeing, especially on sweets, is usually not a good sign.

- Lack of a support group or not meeting with them regularly to compare notes on my journey through life.
- Not getting at least five hugs a day.
- Prolonged periods without cardiovascular exercise.
- Difficulty getting to sleep at night.
- Not taking at least one day off per week. This one can mess me up in a hurry.
- If I can't remember the last time I scheduled a vacation or opportunity for mental rest.
- If I am not looking forward to work on Monday.

Our consciousness is not designed to notice slow gradual changes to our well-being. There have been several times when I had no idea how bad I needed a vacation until I was 100 miles down the road.

In *Think and Grow Rich*, Napoleon Hill writes that, "Through the aid of the sixth sense, you will be warned of impending dangers in time to avoid them, and notified of opportunities in time to embrace them." You gain access to this sense through character development that occurs from by mastering the other twelve principles in his philosophy. Pay attention to messages life is sending you, whatever the source and whatever the form. But remember, sometimes a cigar is just a cigar—not every random event carries a lesson.

CONCLUSION

If you want to get more out of this book, give yourself a reason to do so. Decide to help a high school or college student study more effectively. Find someone who needs your help and agree to find information that will help them. Then pick up this book with the intention of locating information that will help you solve this problem. You'll see ideas you didn't notice before which directly relate to this new problem. In addition, your peripheral awareness will make note of several other ideas in a way that you can come back to them or use them in other situations. Giving yourself a context with which to interact with the information lake called *Brain Dancing* provides your mind with a framework for a useful understanding of the material.

As it is with this book, so it is with life on a larger scale. We are surrounded by an infinite sea of intelligence and information. Our vast subconscious mental processes are continuously scanning this infoscape for ideas relating to the directions we have told our subconscious we want to go. The more precise the direction, the more selective it can be, and the more useful the information it will reveal to you.

The scale of knowledge worker productivity is non-linear. The key to maintaining balance is to operate at peak performance levels as much as possible throughout each day. This will allow you to get so much done during work hours, that taking time off for personal activities justifies itself as a means of maintaining high productivity. In knowledge work, peak performance is accomplished by building specialized capacity via a succession of projects of increasing complexity, cultivating high levels of personal energy, and then directing this skill, knowledge and energy towards a purpose you care about, with all the focused discipline you can muster.

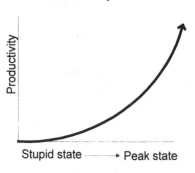

"You are guaranteed to miss 100% of the shots you don't take."

— Jan Schott

Brain Dancing in Five Minutes a Day

This section is for those who like to read books in a more anecdotal fashion. When an item points to a lengthy section, I'm indicating that the material should be skimmed for overall impression, and selectively studied only if time permits. To the right of each item, write notes that address the following two questions: "What do I need to remember?" and "What should I do differently as a result of learning this?" Arrows (➔) have been placed on the specified pages for quick reference.

Chapter 1   **Notes**

❏ Mental leverage is achieved by emphasizing thoughts which have a processional impact on multiple aspects of knowledge work. 9

❏ The incredible diversity of possible thought combinations. 11

❏ Effective knowledge workers identify strategic and generic thinking processes, and then focus their energies on making a few important decisions at the highest level of conceptual understanding. 12

❑ Your mind cannot focus on the opposite of an idea. 33

❑ Utilize the incubation principle by accelerating your confusion rate. 34

❑ A Picture is Worth 1000 Words in Your Mind as Well. 36

❑ Developing your mental visualization muscle is a high leverage use of your time. 37

❑ Discover which submodality shifts work best for you. 40

❑ Pick any object within sight and draw it in detail. 44

❑ Close your eyes and examine the mental picture you have of the project you are currently working on. The image should be how things will look when you have completed the project. 46

❑ Create a metaphor that represents the unique qualities of the project you are currently working on. 48

❑ 24. Say the following affirmation using a variety of physiology's: "My flexible learning strategies help me learn faster." Say it 3 times quietly, 3 times while writing it on a piece of paper, and 3 times while doing jumping jacks. 50

❑ Close your eyes, look upward at a 20 degree angle, and count backward from 100 to 1, in about 2 second intervals. Do everything possible to keep your mind focused only on the counting. 55

Chapter 4   Notes

❑ Tune-in to the flow of ideas in conversations. 63

❑ Mastermind principle. 64

❑ To increase dialogue skills, center your personal security on the degree to which you have aligned your habits with the fundamental principles governing our lives. 67

❑ Think of someone you care about and send them some positive energy. Distance is irrelevant. Imagine them smiling, happy, basking in the sunshine of life. 68

❑ Fluff busting techniques for more precise communication. 82

❑ Use complementary modes of thinking during dialogue - the "Six Thinking Hats" metaphor. 84

Chapter 5   Notes

Chapter 6   Notes

Chapter 8   Notes

BRAIN DANCING ONLINE

Brain Dancing Online (BDO) has been established on the world wide web portion of the Internet to provide you with up to date information related to Brain Dancing. At this site, you have the option of joining a mailing list. This allows me to send out periodic E-mail messages to you announcing new products and features of Brain Dancing Online. There is no cost for this service and you will have the option of removing yourself from the list at any time.

The web site is located at:

http://www.bdance.com/bdance/homepage.htm

My e-mail address is:

mir@bdance.com

FYI: "mir" stands for "Mobilize Intellectual Resources".

BIBLIOGRAPHY

Aguayo, Rafael: *Dr. Deming, The American Who Taught the Japanese About Quality*.

Bailey, Covert: *The New Fit or Fat* and *Smart Eating*.

Bandler, Richard and Grinder, John: *Frogs into Princes* and *Reframing*.

Bandler, Richard: *Using Your Brain* (book and audiotape).

Biro, Brian: *Beyond Success*.

Boar, Bernard: *The Art of Strategic Planning for Information Technology*.

Buzan, Tony: *Using Both Sides of Your Brain, Speed Reading* and *The Mind Map Book*.

Calbom, Cherie and Keane, Maureen: *Juicing For Life*.

Chuen, Master Lam Kam: *The Way of Energy*.

Chopra, Deepak: *The Seven Spiritual Laws of Success* and *Quantum Healing Workshop* audiotapes.

Covey, Stephen: *The 7 Habits of Highly Effective People* (book and audiotape series), *Principle Centered Leadership* and *First Things First*.

Cusumano, Michael and Selby, Richard: *Microsoft Secrets*.

de Bono, Edward: *The Six Thinking Hats*.

Dewey, John: essay in *The Makers of the Modern World*.

Diamond, Harvey and Marilyn: *Fit for Life* and *Fit for Life II*.

Dilts, Robert: *Skills for the Future*.

Drucker, Peter: *The Effective Executive*.

Durant, Will: *The Story of Civilization: Our Oriental Heritage*.

Edwards, Betty: *Drawing on the Right Side of the Brain*.

Emerson, Ralph Waldo: *Compensation* and *Self-Reliance*.

Ferguson, Marilyn: *The Brain Revolution* and *The Aquarian Conspiracy*.

Frank, Stanley D.: *Remember Everything You Read: The 7 Day Evelyn Wood Speed Reading Program.*

Franklin, Ben: *Autobiography.*

Gawain, Shakti: *Creative Visualization.*

Goldberg, Phillip: *The Intuitive Edge.*

Harvey, Paul: various news broadcasts.

Hill, Napoleon: *Think and Grow Rich* and *Law of Success.*

Hittleman, Richard: *Introductory Yoga Video* and *Be Young with Yoga.*

Huxley, Aldous: *The Doors of Perception.*

Jeavons, John: *Grow More Vegetables Than You Ever Thought Possible on Less Land Than You Can Imagine.*

Kirschner, M.D., H. E.: *Live Food Juices.*

Kordich, Jay: *The Juiceman Audio Tape Series* and *The Juiceman's Power of Juicing.*

Loehr, Dr. James E., and McLaughlin, Peter J.: *Mentally Tough* book and *Mental Toughness* audiotape.

Maltz, Maxwell: *Psycho-Cybernetics.*

Mandino, Og: *The Greatest Salesman in the World.*

McCarthy, Michael J.: *Mastering the Information Age.*

McCormack, Mark: *What They Don't Teach You at Harvard Business School.*

McKay, Harvey: *Swim with The Sharks Without Being Eaten Alive.*

Meyer, Christopher: *Fast Cycle Time: How to Align Purpose, Strategy, and Structure for Speed.*

Microsoft Corporation: *Building Client/Server Applications with Visual Basic.*

Murphy, Dr. Joseph: *The Power of Your Subconscious Mind.*

Nightingale, Earl: *The New Lead the Field.*

O'Hanlon, William: *Taproots.*

Ornstein, Robert: *The Psychology of Consciousness.*

Orr, Ken: *Structured Systems Development.*

Peck, M. Scott: *The Road Less Traveled.*

Peters, Tom: *Liberation Management.*

Pilzer, Paul Zane: *Unlimited Wealth* and audiotape of interview with Anthony Robbins available by calling 1-800-445-8183.

Pinckney, Callan: *Callanetics for Your Back* and *Callanetics* exercise video.

Redfield, James: *The Celestine Prophecy*.

Robbins, Anthony: *Unlimited Power* (book and audiotapes), *Awaken the Giant Within*, *Personal Power* audiotapes, *The Five Keys to Wealth and Happiness*, *The Keys to Your Unlimited Success* Personal Power video, *Unleash the Power Within: An Owners Manual to the Brain* video.

Robbins, John: *Diet for a New America*.

Roddick, Anita: *Body and Soul*.

Rose, Colin: *Accelerated Learning*.

Russel, Peter: *The Brain Book*.

Russo, J. Edward, and Schoemaker, Paul: *Decision Traps: The Ten Barriers to Brilliant Decision-Making and How to Overcome Them*.

Schroeder, Lynn and Ostrander, Sheila: *Superlearning*.

Schroeder, Lynn, Ostrander, Sheila and Ostrander, Nancy: *Superlearning 2000*.

Selye, Hans: *Stress Without Distress*.

Senge, Peter: *The Fifth Discipline* (book and audiotape).

Silva, José: *The Silva Mind Control Method*.

Thompson, Charles: *What a Great Idea*.

Toffler, Alvin: *Future Shock*.

Trudeau, Kevin: *Mega Memory*.

Twain, Mark: *Life on the Mississippi*.

von Oech, Roger: *A Kick in the Seat of the Pants*.

Walker, Norman: *Fresh Vegetable and Fruit Juices*.

Wigmore, Ann: *The Wheatgrass Book*.

Wing, R. L.: *The TAO of Power*.

Wycoff, Joyce: *Mindmapping*.

Notes

Notes